PIERCED

PIERCED

Hubert Rondeau

To order additional copies of this book, contact:
Xlibris Corporation
1-888-795-4274
www.Xlibris.com
Orders@Xlibris.com
69058

Contents

I dedicate this book to the one, to the many who come, and dig deep into the soil of their own hearts with, repentance, to sow the good seed the seeds of grace, and come forth with the treasure of Christ within their hearts. Unto the salvation of their souls. Christ alone, the pearl of greatest price. The true treasure, hidden in the field. If you find Him you will know, 'He' is life.

It takes 'more' power to truly humble and save one man
than it would take to make a hundred more universes, like
the very one we are a part of. All of creation obeys its master.

Only men rebel continuously.

I'd have a lot of 'enemies' if people knew me Lord

You'd have a lot of friends if they knew me Son

Act

Act's 17:27 "So that they should seek the Lord, in the hope that they might Grope for Him, and find Him, though He is not far from each one of us.

Lord God I seek you, I need you, I grope in the darkness searching for the light. I crawl about on hands and knees, looking for one who might - lead me to you But there are none to be found, they all have gone their own way, nobody around so as I look for you my saviour I just bow and pray. I grope for you in the darkness, looking every day for the light. I bow before you Jesus the way the truth and the life. My heart I lay upon your altar, a living sacrifice, my body nailed to the cross with you, Now in my Spirit also is life. I look for you each morning, each day and every night, nothing of this earths for me Lord, you are my only life. Nailed upon this tree with you, everything's so clear I can see throughout eternity, the best place to be is here.

My view of all the world is gone, I now see the truth, flesh and blood lead to death,

The Spirit is the life in You. So, drive those nails in deeper, that hold me to this tree, I'll forever linger here, and ever be with thee. My eyes are open wide now, [nothing else can move] But I can see you now so clearly, that all I want to do is stay, stay, stay right here with you, and throw my body on your altar, and hang upon this tree. To the world I'll be a derision, a shame, and a fool, but I know that I have life now, crucified with you.

Now I sit in the dirt, and humbly I know, to be absent from the body is to be present with the Lord.

A Hungry Heart

A Hungry Heart, a thirsty Heart, to breathe the breath of life.
Where shall I go? Look to, 'what' part?
To search and find this precious life.
A Hungry Heart, a thirsty Heart longing, you to see.
In Spirit and in truth, I find your heart so searching Lord, 'for Me'.
Broken now and all alone, No one knows me precious Lord,
loneliness and solitude 'not my choice,' Lord I come to you.
Every day I die again, a thousand times ten thousand.
To be crucified with you my gain, to put down flesh rebellion.
A Hungry Heart, a thirsty Heart, a broken Heart, and contrite.
Oh lord you will not despise! - A Hungry Heart.

Amen

All of thy waves

All of thy waves and billows have gone over me!
Deep calls unto deep. Living water!
Washing over me.
Shattered vessel burst asunder—broken vessel filled again.
Again too deep for wading! Way to fast to drift and float
Too powerful for man, The Mighty Holy Ghost!

Summon all your forces! Angels from on high carry me to that water.
Baptize till I die! Carry me again My Lord, consumed in Holiness,
brought forth by your precious blood. { living water this.}
No more flesh eternal-No more flesh at all . . . I have to you come for Life. I have
heard your call!

A Picture

A picture, Just a reflection of an image, What image comes to your mind
Of the Day that you Stand before the Lord, At the judgment seat of Christ?

Lord I want to be Holy, Your word says Be Holy for I am Holy.
I want to be Holy, I pray again Lord. Consecrate me wholly unto thee.
For you have seen all that I've done, every battle lost, and every battle won,
You have seen my hearts wounds, some put there by self, and some by others too.
You know what I've won and lost, my toil, shame, and pain, I've counted
everything as loss, that salvation I might gain. To me all now is rubbish, and set
out for the fire,

No value in one earthly thing, you are my one desire. All things are for
consuming in the fire of your wrath, cause men would set their hearts on them,
and turn away from your true wealth. For you are all consuming Lord, yet you
are everything, you are my redeemer, you are my precious king. All I have I lay
before you, you are my all in all,
So I come and pray before you Lord hold me close lest I should fall.
There is nothing in the bottom of that pit from where I've come, not one thing of
value
Nothing to bring home. I bring my life to you today, please wash and sanctify,
and make me Holy in Jesus precious blood I pray, and take my sin away remove
from me my life long stain and sanctify me once again. I pray in Jesus name
Amen.

There is nothing else on this earth worth anything at all, but Jesus Christ and
Christ alone
He is the all in all. He is the everlasting one. He is everything to me . . .
Lord sanctify me by your word, your word is truth.

Are we related?

I am indiscriminate, I am juicy, My poisonous words
Bypass minds and hearts, they defile whole persons
With bitter poisons.

I am gossip; my middle name is meddler,
My surname is Talebearer.
My Fathers name is Father of lies.'
And my coach is Belial [the worthless one]

Who am I? I'm the enemy of mankind,
And like the proverbial seductress, I hunt the precious life.
You, even you, can taste of my fruit at any time.
You need only to speak about another what is none of your concern.
Look close, Are we related?

Romans 16 17-18
Now I urge you, brethren, note those who cause divisions, and offences,
Contrary to the doctrine which you have learned, and avoid them. For those who
are such do not serve our Lord Jesus Christ, but their own belly, and by smooth
words and flattering speech deceive the hearts of the simple.
So are we related? Do you tell stories just to be conversing?
Or do you Honour God by speaking righteousness, and truth?

The bible says that Satan is the Father of lies [talebearers, story tellers, liars, and
gossips.]

While the Spirit of truth dwells within all of Gods true children . . .

Mirror time: Who is your Daddy? Really . . . .

As I lay in His pavilion

As I lay in His pavilion, a place of streets of gold clear as crystal,
yet transparent as glass. I could see the stars bellow me, and I shuddered as
I realized where I must be at last! To afraid to look up, I stared upon the scene
below only to feel a loving hand, and hear a voice say to me,
"arise" do not be afraid; for I am your exceeding great reward, the one you've
been waiting for. 'not seeing, you've adored. I thought, Lord, I'm not worthy!
You have known all of my sin.
My son He said unto me, If thus had not been paid, I'd not have let you in!
So get up! Look up! Your redemption is at hand! As He spoke it I got up but
found I couldn't stand. His glory, and His majesty overwhelmed me there, and on
my face I fell again, His beauty I could not bear. I then thought I'd imagined a
chuckle of amused glee'
And I heard His voice again as He said to me, My son, you never knew it, but
this is the reason why I made you long ago, so that you could be here with Me,
and Know as you have been known.

Banter & Brag

They travel together down the same noise some path

Each one boisterous and shouting like a trumpets blast

Not one peaceful moment, not one quiet sound. No, not one at all

With Banter and Brag around.

Tumultuous, and tempestuous, ever is the air. Mighty loud and clamorous

about this noise some pair. Their din you can feel, and touch in the air

Banter& Brag, Banter& Brag the boys from 'anywhere'.

How many are their brothers? How many are their kin?

How many are the family of those who make such a din?

So proud, yes so arrogant each a know it all, never a quiet humble moment

On the Holy one to call. Wonder—such a wonder how ever can this be?

Made in Gods own Image, but rebellious as can be? Know it all, 'disputers'

Argument for everything, never a quiet moment, hush, or prayer, or anything

—Banter&Brag, Banter&Brag

Be careful what you say

*Be careful what you say, while walking in the way, every word you speak, every
claim you make. You must control your tongue, for it is like a sword, which cuts
deep within the hearts of those who hear the word. Do not talk idle-wise, or
vainly, that's not good. The precious words are few, vein babblings, not of God.*

*Let your tongue be clamped down tight between your teeth, so it will not betray
the vanity beneath, for even a fool when he is quiet is thought wise.*

*God see's through every disguise, and nothing from Him is hid. He knows the
deepest thoughts that we try to hide.*

Be not weary in well doing stand ye firm in all
For faith will work a great reward, and keep you from a fall.
Be ye glad when all seems lost, and storms arise within,
For hope and comfort shall prevail, Gods faithfulness
Shall win. Be not weary, but stand firm, this I can attest
That as you go and stand with Him, He'll make you
Pass the test . . .

Having done all to stand, Stand!'

Beseeching word

I beseech you therefore brethren by the mercies of God Not to parrot!
For we are to God the fragrance of Christ among those
who are being saved, and among those who are perishing.
To the one we are the aroma of death leading to death, and to the other,
Life leading to life. For we are 'not' as so many 'parroting', peddling the
word of God! But as of sincerity, as from God, we speak in the sight
of God in Christ. God leading us in triumph in Christ, and through us diffusing the
fragrance of His knowledge in every place.

No parroting, jesus jangling, or whatever you want to call it.
If Christ is in you, you must emit the fragrance of death to those who
oppose themselves, and the fragrance of life to those who are being called to life. If
you are a 'jesus parrot' I suspect that there's not much of
His fragrance in you! [check yourself with God!]

When Jesus is speaking people repent, humble, turn to God,
get mad, reject, hate, or love . . . But when it's jesus jangle, it turns
everybody off. The scripture's say we will be judged for every idle
word. Don't parrot. Dig deep into the wells of salvation, that when you
speak, your words will be fragrant to God, in Christ Jesus. If you love
God with every fibre of your being, you are blessed!
If you Mock [pretend] You alone will bear it.
The Jews wouldn't even say God's name
for reverence, and Honour, and Holy fear of the Lord! We throw Jesus name around
like a dirty shirt, and tag His name onto every vain imagination that rifles through
our heads, and before you know it, we have a basket full of jesus junk, that is none
of His! eesh man! He is HOLY!

Those who come close to God 'must' Honour Him, and every one who
who draws near will be humbled! Father, humble me, even crush me, that I might
decrease, and Jesus increase. Bless you Lord come!

Hayda—sara—bo-to—sou-unday . . . 'You are Holy Lord. You are to
Be feared to the uttermost! There is no-one like you, No, not one!

How do you know that you are not parroting?
You taste and see that the Lord is Good! . . . What? . . . Well,

when you speak there is soundness, richness, purity, grace, power,
love, and all the flavour, and fullness of God comes out in your words.

If you begin to gloat over it, or be proud, His word will stop, and you will revert
to parroting. If you remain humble, and thank Him, and give Him
Honour, you'll get more, and as you cast your crown to the dirt, and throw your
[self] to the ground, He will raise you up. This word is for all
Who would be His, God is no respecter of persons, [no favourites]

BETTER

Better it is to groan in repentance,
than to rejoice in deception!

Better to glory in poverty
than to cry-out for selfishness and greed

Better to languish in affliction than to
sport in vain pleasures!
Better to indulge in intersession
than boast in false numbers

Better to live forever than
to rebel for now!

Better to walk a lonely road
than to run the lane of rebels, yes
better to be alone with God than to
be found in the company of his foes!

Why do you hunger so my heart,
why do you cry out within me?
hope in God for we shall yet praise him
He alone is glorious, and majesty is in
His beauty! AMEN, YES AMEN

Bless you Lord! amen. amen

—*How can I stand here with you, and not be Moved by you? Would you show me how could it be any better than this! Your all I want, your all I need your everything, everything.*

Bless you Lord! Amen, amen! How can I stand here with you, and not be moved by you? Would you show me how could it be any better than this! Your all I want, your all I need your everything, everything.

And, they teach as precept the doctrines of men. So they take my name in vain. "They take my name for nothing." It is powerless and useless to them, because they go their own way as the heathen do who know not God!

Like, Zechariah 5,2

I see a flying scroll, its width is big, and its length is bigger!
I didn't come to bind my children with a dead and killing word!
But to lose them with the Spirit of the word! For the law of the
word kills {by design} to make every man guilty. But the Spirit of
the word gives life! What do you see? I see a scroll!
Its written on both sides, it is the curse that goes over the face of the
whole earth! Every thief is cast out by one side, and every perjurer the other!

Verse 4: I will send out the curse says the Lord of Hosts;

It shall enter the house of the thief, and the house of the one who swears falsely by my name. It shall remain in the midst of his house and consume it with its timber and stones.

-In vain do they worship me teaching as doctrine the precepts of Men.

Hey! I said, Hey! God has revealed the deep [hidden] things of God, to us by His Spirit! For the Spirit searches all things, Even the deep things of God. Which are Spiritually discerned.

-This is driving Me Man! Who has known the Mind of God? We ought to have, and need the Mind of Christ! What do you see Hubert? I see a scroll! They take My Holy name in vain!—Why? They perjure, and they lie! They come to Pretend—they tend, to pretend, and come to naught, cause without My Spirit they are! Repent . . . Man.

Holy Ghost, you are so intense, I could just explode from the inside out! Have Mercy on us wicked un-believers.
We claim Christ, but choose our own ways!

How vile it is to pretend before such a Holy King!
When we aught to bear the cup of the Holiness of the Spirit,
Placing the fragrant wine to His lips, do we not rather bake the bread of our own recipe?
Should our basket not be removed? even our own heads? Hmmm?

O God I can see but I cant touch you! I can see, but Im still blind!
Have mercy! Have mercy! Have Mercy! The warrior of Light wouldnt go into His own house,
nor into His own wife for His own pleasure, while His commander was out in the battle field! Do we refrain from
doing our own pleasure, while the battle rages on?
Do we not serve our own creature, rather than our creator, who
is blessed forever? ---Hmmmm

I prayed God make me real with you. (He said)
Its going to hurt! Yep! It does!
                              Worth it!!
                              Worth it!!

Blessed

Blessed are those who dwell in your House they are ever praising you.
Blessed are those who's strength is in you who's hearts are set on Our God.
They will go from strength to strength till we see you face to face.

Yes! Blessed.

How lovely is your dwelling place o Lord of Hosts,
there's a hunger deep inside my soul, only in your presence
are my heart and flesh restored.

how lovely! how lovely.

How lovely is you dwelling place. O Lord of Hosts.

Thank you Jesus for your grace, your Spirit lives within me.

Thank you. thank you.

OH Lord God: That we might know you, forgive I pray our generations of presumptuous sin.

One I believe is that we are so rhetorical in everything we say and do in the name of Christianity that the world can't see you in us at all!

Maybe that's why lukewarm Christians get no response from anyone when we preach.

Just a thought Lord forgive me I pray for my ignorance of you. Cause you are God and I am nothing.

Still I am glad that you are God Hallelujah! yes, and you save to the uttermost those who come to you, even from the pig pen . . . amen

Hesharra whassae watto stoena!

thank you Jesus for your perfect gift, eternal life. amen.

"But God I Thought"!

I thought you were like me and you did things my way. I thought I was like you, and did things 'my own way.' I thought, It doesn't matter what I do today. "GOD" I thought 'I' was it, 'all that mattered anyway'. I really didn't Know you, and never looked your way. I looked only through my own eyes, and didn't see you there. Your way is so pure and clean. so special and so fine I think I need to change my thoughts, cause none of yours are mine. I think I need to turn around, and think things through again, I'm thinking that I need to know you Jesus as My friend.
                    mmmmm, Just thinkin

Thank you Lord for a good thought.

Covered

You are covered in My blood. Yes, the mighty cleansing flood.
No, not worldly wisdom, small, My blood is great, and all in all.
Powerful to make one whole, to wash and heal you once for all.
My chosen vessels will contain, all I shed to bring them in.
Every drop has paid the cost, none of My precious blood was lost!
Now it covers head to toe, My beloved whom I know.
They'll be with Me one day soon, you can know this, this is true.
How they ache for Me to come. How unto My presence run,
Seeking precious time with Me, how they hunger just to see.
One thing they ask, yes, this they seek, to behold My beauty, and to speak.
No other wonder, no none at all, will they seek, they will not call. These are mine,
with a true heart, they are small and set apart, My eye is steadfast upon them, I'll
not turn away from them.

Dear Dad

Father I decided to sit down tonight, and to write to you this letter. I guess you know that I am fifty now, being my Dad and all. It's shocking to me Dad, that I'm this old. I never thought I'd live this long. Do you still love me? I know that I have brought you much shame, 'living as I did all these years'. I was so ill so much of the time, and so lost and blind as well. I know that I am not the man you wanted me to be, I can tell as I read your letters to me. Father I should have written back to you long, long ago. It's been so dumb of me, it's like I forgot that we are blood. I forgot who I was, and became whom I am not! So when I look in the mirror now, I don't know who I am looking at! Am I the guy that shouldn't be, or is it 'ok' now that I am finally realizing that I have lived in a swine's pen, rather than a palace since my youth? Still Father, coming too myself has been painful. I have spent my nights alone now, I know you know this too. Sometimes I find it hard, but good, I wish I could just see you.

Father sometimes at night, I would like to just get up, and walk right through my roof, to climb the stairs I cannot see, but then run hard, and catch up to you. I know you are walking slowly, just in case I'd come, but I am having major trouble taking steps, Father, even one. I remember peeking in one time, to where you live and dwell, just as quickly as I got a glimpse, out again I was compelled. You said I couldn't linger there I'd have to leave my stuff behind. Nothing of my world belonged, no glory lord was mine. As I sit here at night sometimes, and think of things to come, with all the evil that I've done I've missed my Father's love. Who is there to help me now? I am so despised, as I come and look to you, the people pass me by. My friends and family stand afar, pretentiously they smile as though they really cared.

They don't know me, not at all. As different I am from them all. I look like my brothers, and we sound alike, but inside of us is different. It's always been this way. I lost my way once so long ago, I only want to come Home now, You know that it's so.

Father, my words are so many, I at times talk too much, the people I am around don't want to hear, can't taste, or see, or feel or touch, who you are. Father, please heal my wounded heart, set me free from this world of snares, and help me to Re-start. Father, thanks for not forsaking me.

Love U/R son

Dear Son

Dear Son; Son, People have no desire for the for
things that they have no inkling of. They cannot
Hunger for what they know nothing of! They cannot
thirst for a drink of something they do not perceive,
or a morsel of food they do not know exists, say a
steak or some such thing. Truly they starve because
they do not know what food is! Though you feast right
beside them, they starve next to you, for in them is not
the hunger for life. Thus pray for hunger as you
have before . . .
Son, you need to have more confidence in Me!
Son, I will lead you, and guide your steps. I am
the Lord, you should shout and rejoice,
because you know that you do feast in their
presence, while I feed you, and they famish,
though they don't know it! But pray for them,
even as you revel in Me.

Dimple

My son, truly you are a part of my precious bride.
Like a dimple on her cheek, the part I like to kiss.
You are my treasure.
Oh I love you Father, that's so sweet, so filling,
So—so, what can I say? Come! Kiss me some more,
Kiss me some more, Kiss me again!
Kiss me with your passion for your precious bride,
Your precious one. Kiss me with the kisses of eternal love.
The Kisses of glory, the kisses of God, forever amen!
I'm breathless, my beloved, I'm stunned, and overwhelmed By you. Oh I long for
your Spirit in me. Thank you Father, come and kiss me again;

Love, Dimple

Do you know

Do you know God is not crushed if you don't believe in Him?
That your opinion of Him has absolutely no effect, no effect on Him whatsoever?
Do you know that every unbeliever is more devoutly
religious than God is or will ever be?
Do you know that all of His true Children are believers, and not religious at all?
Do you know that the world's religions are offensive to God and blasphemous
to the cross of Christ?
Do you know that the only way to God is the cross of Jesus Christ, and the only
stumbling block to God is the cross of Jesus Christ?
Do you know that no man can pray to God but by Jesus Christ?
I wondered if you knew?

Every day in every way never miss a minute
Love the Lord with all your heart, and everything That's in it.

Do You Know What Hurts?

Do you know what hurts?
The hurt that will last a long, long time?
Can you even guess what I am about to say?
Do you think I can make it rhyme?
Don't hold your breath, nor clutch you heart, If you are really real,
it's gonna hurt.
Do you know what hurts? when God shows you how many years He gave you
to seek Him with your whole heart, and you suddenly understand that you
NEVER
ever really did!
I am not wrong in this, and this is a condemning fact to almost all of Humanity.
Christians included.

Isha bowisha otasta nomaheo!
Wake Me up LORD! I need to know you!
Please Jesus have mercy on us blind ones.
Please show us your Glory that we might know you and Honour you.
Amen.

D'you want your ears tickled?!

Well God wants to tickle them too! But first He wants to clean them
out, so that His truth will be a delight to them . . . 'your ears'!
Can you imagine, You come close to your sweetheart, to whisper sweetly in Her ear
only to find it waxy, or strewn about with sawdust?
What do you think, when God tries to whisper into our ears and He finds a deaf
ear, and a cold heart? Do you see how we grieve the Holy spirit?

Heb 12; 6 For those who come to God must believe that He is
and that He is a rewarder of those who "seek" Him!

-To be born again; You 'must' believe that God is and that He is a rewarder of those
who seek Him. He's not obligated to reward self seekers, or pleasure Seekers.
-You must believe that He is God, not you! How many I's in G-O-D?
-How many me's in G-O-D? How many But I's in G-O-D?

He says Repent! And be converted. So we twit along like a silly
child singing 'I believe in Jesus' dancing, and prancing, and jangling
about, Man! We don't need the chirp, but we need the sap!
Paul said, the root supports us, we don't support the root . . . the sap comes from
the Root, not the wind! So why do we follow so many winds of doctrine,
And disregard the fact that, there is no sap, and that the root is drying up?

Jesus said that every branch in Me that does not bear fruit will be cut off.
And every branch that does bear fruit will be pruned so that it can bear more
Fruit . . . eeekk, groan, groan, oowwww! That Hurts! Lord! That Hurts!
Thank God when you feel it, and its pruning, you know your not dead.

D'you hear it? Jesus said 'Have salt in yourselves,' I think he meant have Some sap
on tap, some oil in the vessel, and in the vine of your life,
If no one could ever guess that you are a Christian, are you?
I've been rebuked for preaching more than once when I hadn't said a word!
I like that . . . I also like Jesus tickling my ears, I get a mile long grin, and then a
tear and cry, Then beg him to take me Home.

Faith

Faith is the substance. Faith is the stuff.
When your strength is gone and you've had enough.
Faith is the matter of which all is made,
and the glue that will cause you to stay.
When your strength is gone and your body is worn,
your tools are broken and stolen—there's Faith alone.
When the mountains are high and the water so deep,
when you have nothing but a heart that says I believe;
Faith.

Faith

Not an image, or emotion, not a thought,
even of heaven, not a devotion,
not a swirl of spinning, spiralling hopes and dreams,
not a wishful thought or scheme;
But to just be still and know, to trust all to Him.
I know who I believe and I am faithful
that He will keep what I have given to Him against that Day.
Faith.

Faith

I didn't choose to come here, I mean to be born,
My life is not 'my' idea. Of what Lord, was I formed
No doubt I am here though, these words do attest;
It's not about me and in Faith do I find rest.
That He who has begun a good work in me
will complete it until the day of Christ.
Faith.

Faith

Seeing what is not visible, what is, but is not known.
Standing in the truth of God, even though you are alone.
Go out of your Country! Leave your stuff and family behind.
I am sending you to a new land, an inheritance in 'Me' you will find.
Faith.

Father forgive my arrogance

*If every molecule in the fist that I shake at your face were the size of the
universe, It still would be nothing to you!
You are God. Oh that you would open my eyes, and give me strength to stand
before you, and be humbled, and healed Lord.*

Fight for the right

*Fight for the right to be crucified with Christ. Fight for the right
to eternal life.
Fight to the end don't ever give in, the one in the mirror who wants'
lust to win.
Fight for the cross strive to get on, the one meant for you, bought
by Gods Son.
Cling to your tree, don't try to get down, if you live for your flesh, you'll get no
crown.*

Father, what do you want me to write?

You can write about my promises, that to you I've made;
that when your parents reject you, I will take you in.
You can write about my precious blood that I shed for you son.
You can write about being born of God for this gift I've given you.
You can write of glory, and of love for your enemies, for the rejoicing
of your heart when you suffer because of me.
You can write that this world hates you, cause you are not it's own.
You can write that you don't like it here, and cry out to come home.
You can write greater love hath no man, than he lay down his life, for an other
one, a son, daughter, husband, wife, this I've truly done.

You can write of all I've done from start until the end, for I've put in you
eternity, Son you can write again.
You can write with the fire, that I'll put in your pen, my flames will jump
and burn the chaff from the hearts of men.

I will be beside you each and every day, to watch and work my word to you,
and to straight your way. My flame will burn so brightly, that many will be
drawn
they will come to see, just what is going on.
You can write of pure white walls, without and within, of precious blood and
healing
Son, in the presence of the King. Take you pen and bring me glory, take and write
your Fathers name, Take your pen and say that He is Holy! Take your pen son
once again, take your pen son once again, you can write . . . . . Abba, Father.

Fire

There is fire in the house of God, and there is would on the fire.
The wood is all that you would of your own will, apart from the Spirit of God.
All that you would do, all that you would desire, all that you would love, all
that You would want! Your would is His chaff, your would will burn in His
Holy Presence, O would to God that you would burn your own would, and dwell
In His will, rather than your would!

Now will . . . Not my will, but thine be done.
Not my kingdom but thy Kingdom come.
Not my will but thine be done, my will I will
Your way. Jesus please change today,
Put in me that will of thine, that thy will
Be mine, not mine. To will and to work, to
Laugh and to talk, to love and to hate,
In thy will to walk . . . amen

Foolishness?

Well the Fear of the Lord is the beginning of wisdom, and the Knowledge of the Holy one is Understanding . . . what then of the worlds knowledge? God's word says men's knowledge whatever it may be, at best is only carnal, fleshly and temporary . . . and sensual earthly and demonic at worst. Why then do so many professional guru's fancy themselves to be wise? God's word say's if any man thinks Himself wise, let Him become a fool so that He may become wise. And it also says that with all of the wisdom of the world men can never come to the knowledge of God. That is so amazing, that God would show His eternal wisdom to the simple, and the wise go away empty handed, Oh the depths of the riches and wisdom of God. By the foolishness of the message of the cross of Jesus Christ salvation comes to those who dare to step out to take hold of, and live out this foolishness that alone can save forever.

For God so loved the world

John 3:19 : and this is the condemnation, that the light has come into the world and men loved darkness rather than light because their deeds were evil.

What we see in Job is that Men can be fooled into thinking themselves righteous. But when God puts His mirror before our eyes we see clearly that He is God, and we are nothing. Not that he despises us, but we bring destruction onto ourselves because we love the darkness that we dwell in. Through Christ, literally a person may be born again, when we see that we are reprobate, and dead. This is impossible for men, and no one can do this for you. You must realize what the content of your own heart is, and recognize that you cannot stand before an all consuming fire without being burned up. For God is an all consuming fire. How will you stand? Don't despair, turn your whole heart to God, cry out to Him for understanding, and for salvation. He is not willing that anyone perish, but that all would come to Him. But know too, that no man makes a fool of God! He knows the heart. If you or I fool anyone, it's only ourselves.

From The Rising

Scripture says; From the rising of the sun till the going down of the same,
The name of the Lord is to be praised!

And who can know this Lord? The one who created the heavens and the Earth?
The one who declares a thing and it is done?

Who can know such a God as this, a God who has Eyes that see and ears that hear? A
God who dwells in unapproachable light, who bows Himself to look upon the Earth?

He who has clean hands and a pure heart, who has not lifted up his soul to any idol,
nor speaks what is false, He who has a broken heart, and a contrite spirit. This is
the man that the Lord draws near to Him, giving the such a one eyes that see and
ears that do hear. My friends please draw near to this God with all your heart.

Do you realize that God does not care what you think, or of your opinion on
anything at all?
He only looks to see if there is anyone who will humble themselves, and confess
that He is God of all and saves such as are lowly of heart.

Lord Jesus praise be to your Holy name amen. Save your people Lord.

God looks on the heart,
Men look on the look.
scripture says of
Jesus that we are to not look at him
in the flesh, but in the Spirit.

no longer are we to look so to any man,
and if we look to the Spirit of a man its
not long before we see the real man.

We have been taught Lord I give you my heart, even all of my heart. But we
haven't been taught that the heart of man is desperately wicked and evil all
together.

We need not to give Him our heart,
We need to ask Him to destroy our wicked heart, and give us a new heart!

Are you born again?

Hearing they will Hear?

Holiness Is what you look for in your Children O God.
That we would be Holy as you are Holy. How can we draw near to you that we may attain your attribute of Holiness? Even if we climbed the Highest mountain, we would be no closer, nor if we did the greatest of Human feats. All of our thoughts are vein and futile, and our philosophies 'vein deceits' Holiness, Holiness, how far away are you from My heart, O I want to walk with you.
Jesus I know it's only in you that we can be Holy. Lord come into my life and purge me deep within that I might be Holy even as you are Holy amen.

Do you mind that there is a Being one other than yourself, who is greater than all of the universe?

Did you ever consider that the very word Universe means, 'uni' One, and 'verse' sentence?

In the beginning God the creator Spoke the Universe into being! 'Bang!" Let there be, and there was.

Do you mind that God is Spirit, and that He being a Spirit created everything that is, out of things that are not visible?

Do you mind that no matter how minute the particles of matter men will ever see with the most powerful microscopes, they will never see what He, that is God made everything out of?

Do you mind that He, 'God' The creator of the universe is not touched by your opinion of Him?

Do you mind that He is your eternal Judge, even though you claim to 'Not' believe?

I know you believe, you have to. You just choose to rebel so that you can pretend that you are god, and this you don't mind. And neither does He, He knows the truth, and so do you, you are just playing pretend, and I think God doesn't mind.

You may believe that God is an invention of the Mind, I don't mind if you think that . . . we both know the truth. God is Spirit, and all that Know Him, know Him in Spirit and in truth. So even if you do mind God doesn't mind because your mind is not His, and you cant change anything that 'matters' Until you change your mind and bring to your mind that you need Him. Then when you surrender to Him, and come to Jesus Christ, He will give you His mind. Then you will be mind full!

God bless!

Holy.

The universe is multiple light years in expanse. The biggest star we know out there, which is still in our galaxy is Canis Majoris. It is so big that it could contain millions of our suns and many millions Earths.

light travels at 136 thousand miles per second if the universe { uni-single, verse—spoken sentence is, and I believe it is Quadrillions of light years in expanse. That's how many years traveling at the speed of light it would take for you to cross God's single spoken sentence, [the universe]

Now fit this "God" who spoke everything into being into anything that is in your head, mind, thoughts, or imagination! I dare you! Come up with something to explain Him away! you cant do it!

Fit your pet Religious doctrines, or philosophies into this. You cant do it!

God is not 'religious' He is HOLY! completely separate from what He has created the Heavens cannot contain Him. He is separate from His creation.

Think about this, say You are a potter, and you make a miniature Castle. Now, 'Get in it'.—Get in in without destroying it.

Now. You confine yourself to it. "So you say, I can't do anything other than be in this mini Castle which I made".

Is anything happening to your head yet?

How hard is it to walk on Water?
I tell you it's easy! It has to be easier than walking In water,
that's hard especially if there is a current!

I really want to blow your logical mind today.
so that as scripture says we may become fools, that we may become wise.

God is much, much, a zillion time's bigger than everything that He has made. He cannot be conformed, or controlled, nor Manipulated!
Are you seeing anything New yet?

He is Holy . . . He says come out from among them, and be Holy for I am Holy.

Religion, superstition, mysticism, false humility, forms, traditions, and doctrines without the true life of Christ in you. That is—Yeshua Jesus Christ in you the only hope of glory.

These are all damning snare's and severe bondages that keep men from Christ.

God created the heavens and the earth. He is separate from them, in that they cannot contain Him at all. He says that there are more stars in the heavens than all the sands of the earth.

And yet we try to jam Him into our little boxe's to make ourselves feel good, or whatever!

I will tell you with all my heart, even in tears. He will blow your whole box apart and if He saves 'your' soul He will first break your heart.

That's the only way for men to be real with God.

Every person born into this world is very religious.
Every religion out there yours included is all about 'you'.

This is imposible to hear unless the Lord Himself breaks through your darkness and reveals these things to you. Throw yourself down and cry out to Him to show you what you must do to be saved.

If you want to know that these things are true—Just think.

And God will reveal it to you.

It's all about you Jesus.

Holy God you are God thank you for life.

Father thank you for all that you have given to us sinful men through the blood
of Jesus Christ your Son.
Your word says that you have made men upright but they have sought out 'many'
schemes.

No doubt about that in me Lord. I am like Paul in that I am the greatest of sinners
and In no way can I boast, or be unashamed, except that while I was yet a sinner,
like all men, you sent your son. In the likeness of sinful flesh to redeem me from my
sin. Thanks Lord thank you.

I pray for all who would look upon these words that Your Holy Spirit would convict
them of their sin, and bring them to your cross, which is their cross, and that you
would crucify each one who comes to you in truth. Lord walking with you in Spirit
and in truth is the Hardest thing that any human will ever do! But it is also the
'Only" thing worth it in the end. I pray Jesus for many disciples to truly come, repent
for life and be converted in Jesus Holy, and matchless name I pray amen.

Hope
Hope that springs eternal deep within my heart
Jesus Lord and Saviour you are the greater part
Hope that springs eternal stronger everyday
Jesus Lord and Saviour you are the only way
All I am is yours Lord You are my all in all
and I know that you will catch me if ever I should fall
Hope that springs Eternal you are everything to me
And now my Lord and Saviour I pray you set me free

With grace and love I come to find my son's
the broken weary little ones.

With grace I come to find you there'
all alone stripped torn and bare.

With grace I bring Salvation to
all who come and cry unto.

With grace I come Salvation to
Eternal life to bring to you.

My way is straight my love is pure, it is separate from this world of yours.

With grace I come and offer you that you be made anew . . .

How do you 'know' that you Believe?

2 Corinthians 8:15

As it is written, He who gathered much, had nothing left over, and he who gathered little had no lack. 8:14 but by an equality, that now at this time, your abundance may supply their lack, and their abundance may supply their lack, that there may be equality! If Gods minister to your spiritual needs, ministers to your Spirit, is it not right and proper for you to minister to His human needs?

Equality is Spiritual, and physical in this matter. Consider this okay? A wealthy person is lost in the wilderness, or even in the city, with no way out. Then some poor man comes and takes Him by the hand and leads Him out to safety. Will He be so glad that He brings that man to McDonald's? Or if He is wise, will He not share abundantly of His wealth which He would have lost anyway! The real treasure of wealth is like a smile! Its useless until you give it away. But when you give it away, it comes back it comes back to you through many others. The gift of prophesy is not for the possessor of the gift, but for everyone who would avail Himself of it. And the prophet must give all. The more freely He gives, the more He receives. Same with money it's a gift of the Spirit, but not for the receiver to build His own Kingdom, nor to horde, it's for them to freely give, and more will be added. I think that God may have to do some tearing away from selfish receivers in the body, so that they might learn that it's not for them alone! I've known for years in the body that the poor give more to the poor than the rich ever do. They trust in their riches, deny God, and spite the poor of the same body to which they are a part.

The body of Christ is like two hands clasped together, to make one. Not both hands clamped together onto whatever you may believe is yours. So, do you know whether you believe yet? I'd like to change the spelling of belief to by-life, because what you really believe shows up in your life. If you believe that your money is yours, and that it was earned by you and for you, you will keep it and bless yourself. If however you know that it is a gift of God, to be able to gain wealth, for His purpose, and as a ministry opportunity for you, you will use it to minister to the ones He sends your way. Thus ministering to the body of Christ, which you are a part of. If the eye says 'because I am not a foot I am not of the body, does that make it less of a part of the body? If the rich of the body say because she is poor she is no one of us, Be very careful!! You are about to spurn your maker!!

If she is poor, and you rich, that's your fault! If you don't freely give, you remain aloof of the very body that you are to be a part of. If you want another look brother, or sister consider this, and may God give you vision. Scripture's say that money is a defence; Well what about money as a cover, or a coat, a nice warm winter coat? And you could cover the whole body, but you choose instead to cover you, while the bride, the rest of the body remains uncovered? If the prophet gives all, and holds nothing back His gift will never testify against Him. If the prosperous withholds for [Himself] as Ananias, and Sapphira did in Acts 5, Will not their gift testify against them? If I have the gift of prophesy and understanding, but do not give it to you, your sin is on me. But if I tell you as plainly as I can, your blood is on you. Yes you can rob God, by claiming as yours what He gave you to freely give! 2 Corinthians 8:9 For you know the grace of our Lord Jesus Christ that though He was rich, yet for your sakes He became poor that you through His poverty might become rich. Scripturally speaking, it is the poor who are rich in Spirit, and the rich who are poor, what a wonderful opportunity for an awesome Spiritual trade! Ananias and Sapphira missed it! And multitudes of Christians miss it too.

Ahhh what shall we do you say? Give and you shall receive. Pressed down shaken together, and overflowing shall be poured into your bosom. I think the Lord meant of the Spirit as well as, physical, maybe even more so. By Jesus Christ's command there is to be no schism, or division in the body, and no one who owns anything is to own it to themselves. Lest they by-life not!

How can I preach to you the good news, until I can preach the Bad news, which is truly the best news. That is, 'You' are not God! And it's not about you! [That's good news]. If it was about you, you would ruin it, because of 'yourself'. The good news is, You are not God, God is! The Good news is, it's not about you it's about God! That's good news. The good news is if you ever get this, you will have opportunity to humble yourself, and repent, and willingly submit your everything to God. That's good news. The good news is this is not pretend! The good news is that you are His private property, [even if you don't like it]. The good news is that God is not your puppet, and He is not impressed with or by you. The good news is He is way to awesome to be swayed by human pride, and arrogance. The good news is He is so pure, and so, so sweet! The good news is, He is so merciful! [Not stupid] He has no mercy for those who deceive, with emotions, self-pity, and performances. That is snake like. His mercy is on His children. The good news is He brings joy in the morning. The good news is God is real, and He is the rewarder, and the reward of those who diligently seek Him, with all their heart. The good news is Jesus Christ and Him glorified. The good news is God! The good news is God is Holy, undefiled, and separate from sinners. The good news is God has no opinions, He is truth! The good news is He has no points of view, He is Life. He has no arguments to make with men, He is God! The Sun, Moon, and the Stars obey Him instantly, they know their masters voice! The good news is He is able to save to the uttermost all those who truly come to him. The good news is God knows his own, and is able to save his people from their sin. The good news is God you are My God. That's good news, that's very good news. The good news is, If this is good news to you, it's Great news.

*How do you know that
you know Him?*

His voice, 'My sheep hear my voice'

what does His voice sound like?

The thunder.

Yes the thundering of the still small voice { you hear it}

He makes sure that you do. So stop and listen.

The silent voice that shatters things inside of you.

*the thunderous still small voice that when the prophet Elijah
heard it He hid his face in his mantle.*

*The thundering still small voice that you are hearing as you read these words
Listen!*

*The Father spoke from on High once and said of Jesus
'THIS IS MY SON HEAR HIM'*

My sheep hear my voice.

LISTEN!

How Many Sheep

How many Sheep can a shepherd Keep?
How many can a man own? There is one shepherd He is Christ the sheep are 'all'
His own.

He calls His own by name for they know His voice. The voice of a stranger they
will not follow.
So little lambs listen close.

How to Humble

That at the name of Jesus, every knee should bow, of those in heaven, and of those
on earth, and of those under the earth.
What does it take to humble a man? Oh Jesus, Oh Jesus, you know!
Every knee in heaven bow's at the name of Jesus.
We mere men are so proud! No way will we bow the knee!
We bow the head, to make them see,
We bow the head but not the knee, and what about the heart?
Do we ever really bow at all?
Having a form of Godliness, but denying its power,
of such as these turn away.

Consider what it takes to humble a man.
Most men are not humble, but quite proud.
Often even the poorest poor are very, very proud.

Pride comes before a fall, and a haughty Spirit before destruction.
What should I do to North America? What judgment should I bring to hand?
Lord what did you do in times past to such a people, such a land?

Yeremiah, why don't you weep for the daughter of your people?
Do you not see her brazen forehead, That she cannot blush? Jeremiah,
why do you not mourn for the sister, and for brother, do you not see the place,
to which they rush?

They say they are my people, but choose none of my ways.
They cannot kneel before me and be humbled, far from that these days.

Proud and self directed, they consider these their strengths, yet calling themselves Christian, to the very end! Son what should I do to such a folk as this? They take my name but not my cross, they do nothing for the homeless, lame, the sick or for lost! For the orphan or the widow, they just do not care. You'll scarcely ever see a Christian, near any in despair!

They put on lovely masks, and pretend in many ways, but never do I see them groan in any Godly ways. What does it take to humble a man you ask? For many their own grave!!

Hubert's IF

If you lower your standards as to Gods righteousness at all, you end up in the manure pile. Jesus said, if anyone who puts his hand to the plough, then turns back he is not fit for the kingdom of God. In order to plough a straight furrow you must look straight ahead!

As you turn to look back you turn from your target,[the other side]. I have set my sights on the level of righteousness that Enoch lived! He lived it for a long time, 365 years! And God's only reason for taking him up 'alive' was that his righteousness was pleasing to God!

I want that level of righteousness pounding in my veins, burning in my heart, and blowing across the whole landscape of my life! The level of the love for God that Enoch had set in his heart. It was in all of his life, to be pleasing to God, therefore God took him! "Lord" you soon ought to take me, shouldn't you? And God saw Enoch, called him righteous, and took him home. Home to the Father's house. The bible says that Enoch was not, for God took Him.

Don't set your sights high on Sunday, and let them fall into the pit tomorrow. A prophetess?, told me once, You don't have to be like Enoch you know.—I saw a woman who once lived fervently for the Lord, as she turned to other stuff, to foul language, become nearly repulsive, becoming totally different than she had been before. Don't drop the high standard that Jesus Christ purchased for you! That is to trample His blood under foot, and He said that if we lose our saltiness, how shall we be seasoned? but then are worth nothing but to be trampled underfoot by men, on the dung heap. Ouch man! Ouch! But Jesus said it!

Who do you serve? And how do you taste to God? Does He savour the flavour of your life? He says O taste and see that the Lord is good. Guess where you are right now. Yep, in his mouth, don't you see it? He tastes to see if you are good, or, if He should spew you out! Aaaaaaaagh!—No Lord not me! I fast twice a week. I-I-I do all kinds of wonderful stuff for you. I am not like this other son of yours . . . . I know what you think, No it's not scripture. BUT, it is visionary picture language which does apply and reflect the scripture as written.

We must not think that we can either change or set the standards of the gospel of God! We didn't set them in the beginning.—GOD did! God did not give us the bible so that we could use it to prove which one of us was right, and which one of us was wrong. No He gave it to us to show us that He is right, and that the rest of us are just guessing!

The high standard of God's righteousness has been set, and the price to secure it forever has been paid. Jesus blood paid it.

Genuine humility is a good place for us to start, because without humility, we cannot see that no one can change it at all, only accept it, or reject it. Then in the end receive the just reward for your choice. Oh Lord Jesus I do choose the high and Holy standard of the cross as it is, and as your Holy Spirit has revealed it to me. Help me I pray to get on the cross and there to stay. Amen

*Words cannot conceive, or contain,
the Glory of Christ Jesus within a man!
He is so different! Deep, deep within, no one can explain!
He only wants to go Home, to be near His Fathers throne,
for Him to live is Christ, and to die is gain!!*

I can see it

I can see it but I can't touch it, and you want me to be clothed in it. O the pearl of
greatest price, the glory, and the righteousness of Christ.
You said I am come to give you life and that more abundantly, this is eternal life,
the life of the Spirit of Christ in Me.

I can see it but I can't touch it bogged down by this worlds thinks.
My mind a whirling mass of clutter, of chaff and other things.
I can see it but I can't touch it, what Lord shall I do? My mind is split in
half Lord, double minded too! too many things upon me, this world is such a snare.
I want to live for Jesus only—my focus, love, and heart always and forever there.
How then shall I come to you and bridge this wretched gorge? How, O how Lord
Jesus, I want to know you more!

To seek you and to know you, to walk with you is life. To know you
and to love you in Spirit and in truth. To live the life eternal, to kiss The Son and
live, to circumvent His anger by living just for Him.

If we should walk in Him greater things than these to do we'd surely
walk on water, heal the sick, raise the dead, give sight to the blind, and preach the
gospel too.

The Spirit is life, the flesh profits nothing. Lord set us captives free,
and purge our minds with Holy fire, turn us back to thee. Take this worlds cares
and deeds, and crucify them to us, that we would live in Christ alone, and snares
not hang onto us.

Kiss the Son lest He be angry, and you perish from the way,
when His wrath is kindled but a little, blessed are they that
put their trust in Him. Serve the Lord with fear and rejoice
with trembling, no more lukewarm walk with Christ, for He
is everything . . . .

I dont know How

I don't know how to come in, or go out.
Don't know where to put my foot to tread.
I only know that Jesus name is the pillow
On which I rest and lay my head.
Don't know many great and wondrous things,
Don't really understand this place.
I haven't found in many days a way to beat this human race
I know that Jesus is the way, that He alone is life, I know that
There is no other, and that His gate is precise.
I wouldn't want to trade at all the Glory of my Lord, not even for the
World's great treasures, that those who have cannot afford.
The price is way too high, and the cost, 'eternity'.
Lord I just want to live in you, heal my heart, and set me free.
For whom the Son sets free is free indeed.
The way is narrow, the gate is straight. So don't you come
When it's too late. When Jesus closes it, it is done, won't re-open for anyone.
So come right now. Your will to spite, even if you cry all night.
Seek Him there, and tarry long until He comes to you.
I know I don't know everything, but Jesus is both Lord and King.
He is the living sacrifice, there is no other one.
The way is hard and a lonely road, but it is the only road there is.
Many travel all their life, and end up in the wrong place. They didn't look
For the gate, didn't see the way, O, they may have used the saviours name,
But, only in vain. Please my friend look again, and cry out to Him, realize no alibis, or
Excuses work with Him. Just come. For those who come to God must believe that He is,

and that He is the rewarder of those who diligently seek Him. [He is the reward]

For to know Him is Life

*I know that I'm a soldier, though this is not my war. I know that I've been drafted,
but the battle is the Lord's.*

*The affairs of this wicked world don't matter anymore. I'll sleep just outside my
master's gate waiting for my Lord,*

*How can I do any other, even finding my own pleasure while my master wages
battles for my eternal soul?*

*As He says to me watch and pray lest you fall into temptation. And fall away
from the Lord.*

If you don't mind

Do you mind that there is a being one other than yourself, who is greater than all of the universe? Did you ever consider that the very word Universe means, 'uni' one, and 'verse' sentence?

In the beginning God the creator Spoke the Universe into being! 'Bang!" Let there be, and there was. Do you mind that God is Spirit, and that He being a Spirit created everything that is, out of things that are not visible?

Do you mind that no matter how minute the particles of matter men will ever see with the most powerful microscopes, they will never see what He, that is God made everything out of? Do you mind that He, 'God' The creator of the universe is not touched by your opinion of Him? Do you mind that He is your eternal Judge, even though you claim to 'Not' believe?

I know you believe, you have to. You just choose to rebel so that you can pretend that you are god, and this you don't mind. And neither does He, He knows the truth, and so do you, you are just playing pretend, and I think God doesn't mind.

You may believe that God is an invention of the Mind, I don't mind if you think that we both know the truth. God is Spirit, and all that know Him, know Him in Spirit and in truth. So even if you do mind God doesn't mind because your mind is not His, and you can't change anything that 'matters' until you change your mind and bring to your mind that you need Him. Then when you surrender to Him, and come to Jesus Christ, He will give you His mind. Then you will be mind full.-God bless!

IF you Met GOD

If you met God what would Happen to you?

If He suddenly tore open the heavens right above your head and touched you just hard enough to get your attention, What would Happen to your Mind.

He says in Hebrews that yet one more time He will Shake the Heavens and the earth, so that the things that might be shaken may be removed, and those things that cannot be shaken may remain.

Only those things that are His cannot be removed, and How many of His things dwell in your Heart, and life? Just asking? check it out . . .

Do you know Him? Does He know you? What do you say of the Lord? What would He say to you?

I never Knew you!

You were always watchin Me!
I never Knew you, In church, I didn't "see"
All the brothers and sisters the ones who were ever there,
They always said the right things, Hmmmm, Well, Jesus, did 'one' care?
It's been a few years now since I've left that family, I'd gotten sick, and been
Divorced, did anyone call out to Me? I used to go in throng with them, always
would I share, I prayed for them and spoke to them, and yet I'm not aware that
anyone remembers me, I must be quite small, not one brother came my way, not one
sister called, I was always in among them? what's that all about? For eight years
or so they'd seen my life, and, seen my fruit, They had seen my all. I guess I should
know they loved me, And maybe love me still. I'd always heard Christians shoot
their wounded, But I am alive still. Maybe It's just that God wouldn't let them
come and do me in, So that someday maybe By his grace He'd heal, and raise me up
again. So where am I going, and what more can I say? Well, God has given us this
work, to bring us back to Him again.

If you brother falls, who should be there first? Should you? Since you know its you,
just bring him a squeaky little Jesus verse, or Give him you best Shirt? I said I never
Knew you Lord, maybe I'm not alone, Maybe there are less than we think who'd
drag a wounded body home, or to an inn, and pay for everything for Him, until his
wounds without, and in, are healed and he could bear his own load again . . . .

confession . . .
Out on a walk last night on a gravel road, I threw down my stuff, My truck,
My watch, my glasses, my shirt, my under shirt, and my wallet. And I renounced
this world. I confessed God till my voice went raspy and my throat hurt, still today
fifteen or so hours later it still hurts. I shouted to God. I screamed to God. I preached,
and violently repented, kneeling on the gravel, and then lying on my back looking
up into the sky talking to God.

I was seeing as it were, a thousand years of time. I cant explain it, you just need to get
there if you haven't yet. I saw that a man or woman could spend all their lives 'saying'
I honour you Lord, and even shouting I honour you Lord, and Never really honour
Him at all! And just the same sing I praise you Lord, even Jesus my Lord and King,

and never praise Him in anything . . . . I never knew you!—Part of Me was missing,
There's some place inside of me that needs the programming of my eternal King. I have
had many downloads, Always learning, but I feel as though I've been gutted out.
And life's been just a show. I never tried to impress, or fool any one, Wow, Lord help
Me Jesus what have I done? Can someone help Me? I have some-thing's amiss
I need a new operating system, or hard drive I guess, or maybe just a true hug or
two and a Fathers kiss. Or some true love from another part of . . . Christ's Bride.
I know that you can't See me but I just shrugged my shoulders there, wondering,
just wondering, will ever anyone truly care?

I problems?

John 9:2-3 Jesus finds a blind man, blind from birth. His Disciples ask Him, who sinned this man or His parents, that he was born blind?

Jesus Squashed their philosophical assumption, [that in order for a person to suffer some one must have sinned] Saying neither. But that the works of God should be revealed in him.

I was not born either physically, nor was I spiritually blind when I was young. I like Paul says in Romans 7:9 I was alive once without the law, but when the commandment came, sin revived and I died. I see too that when the commandment came sin revived, and I died. And that which was to bring life to me brought death.

I was not born blind, but became blinded by the religiosity, and the forms, and the traditions, lusts, and perversions of this world.

Your society is an all encompassing snare. It truly is. It leads to every form of spiritual bondage through idolatry, and self worship. What is one of the latest mantra's that is being so over used today? [It's all about me] Is it really? Yes it is for most people. Then for some it's even more deceptive the Idolatry showing up as [It's all about My little Johnny, or It's all about My little Suzy].

This is way beyond the house, the car, the material things that people lust for.

Why can't you hear God?—Maybe because, your god is you.—your god is your kids.—your god is lust.—Your god is covetousness.—your god is pride, [church, family, house, sports all that.]—your god is your belly.—your god is pleasure.—your god is what 'you think' [your mind].—or you god is your will.

Like Satan you have I problems. [Isaiah 14: 13-14] For you have said in your heart, I will ascend into the heavens. I will exalt my throne above the stars of God. I also will sit on the mount of the congregation on the farthest sides of the north. I will ascend above the heights of the clouds, I will be like the most High!

Stop now. and think, do you have I problems?

Scripture's say "seek wisdom" God's wisdom, and get understanding.

Understand this, God will not spare, or redeem anything that you have, not even your clothes. Jude says snatch them out of the fire 'hating' the garments defiled by the flesh. Everything in your life,—which you live for other than Christ Jesus, will be His delight to burn.

Do I have I problems? Maybe I do, lets see. Once I cold see hear and touch in spirit, and in true truth the things of God, as a little child. I remember at a young age, maybe 10 or 11, looking everywhere in my parents house. For three days, for something special that I had lost. But I could not remember, and therefore did not know what I was looking for. Right around that same time, maybe just a few days before or after, I either in a dream, or in a vision heard the voice of God speaking to me. I still can see myself looking at about eleven o'clock toward the ceiling in my room, from where the voice came. This voice was not an earthly language at all but a heavenly language, and I understood it completely. It was full of everything wondrous. The next day I remembered the voice, but could no longer remember the message or the words spoken to me. Do you think maybe 'this is what I was looking for, for those three days?' What I was looking for was the Most special treasure ever! And little boys have many treasures, a favourite rock, a pocket knife with a broken blade.

What was I looking for? What was the treasure?

The Kingdom of God is like precious treasure hidden in a field, who when a man finds it, he goes and sells all that he has and buys that field.

Where, who, or what is your treasure? Are you sure that your treasure is not your "I's"?

The Demon possessed man said, what have I to do with you Jesus? Have you come to torment me before the time?

Do we have eyes that cannot see, and ears that cannot hear, and hearts that do not understand, that we might turn to Him? Jesus says if you're I causes you to sin pluck it out, and cast it from you it is better for you to enter life lame or maimed that having both eyes to enter into hell! And if you right hand causes you to sin cut it off, for it is better to enter into live lame or maimed, rather than to have both, and be cast into hell!

Do you have hand, I co-ordination? Are they together designing for you a red hot future?

I would to God that you and I could hear this word and take it to heart.

Lord Jesus in Ephesians you tell us through Paul to WAKE UP! arise from the dead and Christ will give us light. Lord please wake us up we can't seem to do it, and your word says unless a man is drawn by you specifically they cannot come. Please Lord draw us I pray in Yeshua's mighty name amen.

I saw the Light

I saw a light once long ago, what a great light and Holy glow. Your glory shone all around, and I knew I was on Holy ground.

My heart was shattered from such a shame, my life of sin, now was so plain, yet through it all I saw your light, I saw your mercy lord that night. My life has been so hard, and sore, how can it be that you are with me Lord? Such pain, and sorrow, twists, and snare, paths of darkness everywhere. Alone in silence, here I sit with brokenness my only fit; a broken heart and mind you know it's true, it seems to be my road, you knew. You knew I'd be here on this day, you saw it Lord from far away. What must I do Lord to be saved, to have your blessing, joy, and grace.

—*I want you to write for Me, For Me Son! I'd be glad to Father, I'd be glad to.*
I could write about pig pens and being hungry
I can write about spending my life in immorality
I can write about wasting my inheritance on pleasorous living
I can write about the blind, and the leaders of the blind
I can write on being hungry I can write on being poor
I can write about satan stealing my life, by lying to people about me,
then having people lie about me to others too
I can write about a broken wounded body, and a heart that cries out to you Lord
I can write of being lonely, even in a room that's filled!
I can write about being lost, like a little child all alone, when everyone around doesn't
Care, and no one will take him home.
I can write about a sick child, alone and rejected by them all, mocked
and teased for being
Dumb, and not able to play ball.
I can write about a little boy now grown into a man, who doesn't know one thing to do
that will turn out right again! I can write about that child who doesn't know,
who I am.

I wonder

*I wonder what we think sometimes, about Jesus words and His commandments.
It seems to me like we are so spellbound by our own thoughts and desires, and
probably delusions that we perceive His commandments to be mere suggestions,
and opinions.*

*What a Horror! to be this way. He is the Holy Son of the Holy Father who created
everything with his speech. What can you and I speak into being out of nothing?
Yet we esteem Him so lightly, probably because we can see and feel, and touch
ourselves, and not Him.*

*Here is a big clue, be glad that right now you can't see Him because in your present
state if you could see Him His Holiness alone would kill you. That doesn't make
Him evil it proves you are.*

*I don't say you, to exclude Me, I only say you so that you know I mean you as
well, and don't exclude you.*

*He said unless a grain of wheat falls to the ground and dies it is by itself.
but if it falls to the ground and dies it will produce a crop.*

*He said If any man tries to save His life he shall lose it, and if any man losses his
life for His sake and the gospel sake He will find it again.*

*He said take up your cross daily and follow Him.
He said straight is the gate and narrow the way that leads to life, and there are
few who find it.
He said because broad and easy is the path of destruction there are many who find it.*

*Something I have found in My life is that when I am reading, and hearing, and
listening to God's word I feel like I am coming Home, and I am drawn that way,
and It makes me glad!*

For your sake I ask 'Is this the case with you?' Or do you find all of this not
wholesome and drawing, and compelling at all?

Our favourite place to dwell while we live here should be on our own cross.
for if we are crucified with Christ, we have no worldly desire, and we live in the
Spirit, and put no confidence in our own flesh.

Dead men and women don't want anything. They don't covet anything or anybody.
and they have no trouble with lusts of any kind!

When we are Christ's He really does dwell in us, and He really is everything to us.
He is the food we eat [not bread or steak] but our daily bread which is hundreds of
times more desirous than meat or bread, or vegetables.

If you are His He knows it, and has plans for you. 'your sanctification'
that you might bear lasting fruit.

Oh the riches of God that He can change rebels into princess amen.
If every molecule in the fist that men shake at your face were the size of the universe,
it still would be nothing to you! You are God. Oh that you would open our eyes
and then give us strength to stand before you to be humbled by your Majesty and
Glory, then be healed.

If only I could touch the hem of His garment I would be healed!
The scriptures speak of the Lord as the one who
was, and who is, and who is to come.

Think for a moment if He was to come crashing into this wicked and rebellious
world where would we be? What would happen to us?

God is a consuming fire. How do you and I do in the face of a small fire?
The fear of the Lord is the beginning of wisdom, and the knowledge of the Holy
one understanding.

He is coming, Hebrews says Yet one more time He will shake the heavens and the
Earth, that the things which may be shaken be removed, and those things which
cannot be shaken may remain.

One thing only cannot be removed that is Christ in you the Hope of Glory.
Everything else in you, and in the entire world can and will be both shaken, and
removed.

If only you could touch the hem of His garment!

Everything in your life is subject to God period. Like it or not.

This world belongs to Him.

He is the one who was [here,] and who [is here,] and who will come [here] again.

He is not coming to be subject to you or me, or to any man, city, people or nation.

If only you could touch the hem of His garment!

Your mind would be blown!

And you would see how lost and depraved we have all been, then you

would likewise cry out for the rocks to fall on you to hide you from the wrath of the Lamb,

or you would cry out for mercy. Saying save me Lord the worst of sinners.
Jesus did not have to stir up hype, or conjure up anything.
He knew who He was, and His Father within Him. [If my word abides in you, and you abide in my word, we the Father, and the son will dwell in you. As the Father has sent the Holy Ghost also to dwell in us! [what's wrong with us!] How can we be so Godless, and so irreverent, so callous to God and to others? How can we be so powerless in this perishing world, where we aught to shine as 'lights' If God dwells in you why do you love the world and its things, and know nothing of the Holy seed that will bring you up into the eternal Glory? If the one who created the Heavens and the earth lives in you why don't you talk to Him, since He lives in you, And receive from Him words of Gods wisdom, guidance, knowledge, and the power to live a Godly life?

When Paul told Timothy stir up the gift that is in you by the laying on of my hands, do you think he meant hype it up, jingle, and jangle, and conjure up some hypnotic, exciting thing?
Or do you see that He meant, Stir up the deep, deep things of [praying earnestly, seeking the Fathers heart, and walking in the Glory of the Lord that liveth in Him and in us?

We are gutless and powerless because we do not believe,
And we always grieve the Holy Ghost who waits to lead us into
all truth! O lord deliver us from sin and self which is idolatry

as well. Give us new hearts to love the Holy Ghost and new ears to Hear, and hear
with, then give us the tenacity, the zeal and the fire of God inside that Christ Jesus
may dwell in us, your, people richly and truly amen. Father forgive us we are truly
an idolatrous, and adulterous people Deliver us of this thing I ask Jesus in your
name Start with Me amen!

Its because of your Mercy that I, that we are not consumed,
Hebrews says Our God is a consuming fire. Lord Jesus Kill in
Me everything that grieves you, and every lust and every kind
Of sin I pray do it today. Amen. I just want to live for you . . .

Just a little vision

Just a little vision, that kind of amazes me. Seeking God in prayer crying out to Him.
You know the classic prayer. Lord I give you my heart I give you My soul,
I live for you alone. [I give you My heart?] I could see someone, as it were tearing their
heart out to present it to God, and this amazing thought came to Me! Why would you
want to offer something so deceitful, and desperately wicked to our God, who is Holy?
as though you were offering Him some sort of treasure! Didn't Paul say 'this is a trustworthy
statement, worthy of all acceptance, that God came into the world to save sinners,
of which I am chief'? That's pretty much what He said alright.

We need to get beyond this spellbound Christianity that is bound with romanticism,
and twisted emotionalism, with Systematic domination! 'truly a powerful cord of
three strands' not easily broken! Your heart has nothing of value in it at all, apart from
true repentance, day in and day out. Which is why Paul said 'I beat my body to keep it
under subjection, lest after I have preached to others, I find myself rejected.

Paul didn't ask Jesus into His heart on the Damascus road! He rather cried out, who
are you lord? He had an encounter with God! with Jesus! Lord burn everything in me
that is not pleasing to you! amen. Save me I pray! Jeremiah said the heart everybody's
heart is desperately wicked, evil and deceitful, who can know it?
What have we been teaching each other??

It's all about 'me' Lord, come into—My—heart, and be—My—saviour.
He wants to destroy your evil heart, and give you a new heart!—You must be born
of the Spirit! The Spirit is life, the flesh, including the heart profits No—thing!

When one is born again, God gives them a new heart! When you are born again, your heart is pierced, with Christ's spear, and you get a heart transplant. When you've had a heart transplant Christ is more to you than everything, or anything, or anyone! 'Fact!' Don't ask Him into your Heart! That won't help cause it's still your heart! Ask him to give you His heart instead, and while you're at it ask for His mind also, that you might have the mind of Christ. I would caution you though, if He gives you His heart and Mind, your stuff won't be yours anymore, it'll be His, and He'll maybe for the first time in your life with Christ require you to give your very best for the very worst, but that won't matter cause it's not yours anymore anyway, it's Christ's right? We need to wake up! We need to shake off the cloaks of self! we all need to repent and seek him, groping in the dark of this generation until we are able to truly put on the Lord Jesus Christ! And not be conformed to this world any longer, but be transformed in the Image of the stature of the fullness of Christ!

Lord light the fire of your holiness in my heart, my soul, and my body, Make me holy as you are Holy. Lord I believe in you. You are everything to me. Hold Me close, my heart aches with longing for your touch even your Caresses. You are the lover of my soul and this my heart knows very well. Draw nigh unto me, as I hunger thirst and cry out for you to rescue me from this World, I love you Lord, but I'm pretty sure that my love is pretty shallow compared to Your love for me. Lord don't leave me to myself, but come, please come-my heart, even my very life, depend on you.

1 John 5:18 We know that whoever is born of God does not sin; but he who has been born of God keeps himself, and the wicked one does not touch him. We know that we are of God, and the whole world lies under the sway of the wicked one. And we know that the son of God has come and has given us an understanding, that we may know him who is true; and we are in Him who is true, in His Son Jesus Christ. This is the true God and eternal life. He who has been born of God [keeps himself] and the wicked one does not touch Him.

Lord help me to do this, to keep myself, and that it would not be burdensome, or hard at all, even to stand firm against all the wiles of the devil, knowing that the whole world lies under his sway, and that I have fallen into his stuff, Help me Lord to reject this world completely and to live in and for you. Amen.

Lord, Who may ascend your Holy mountain? Who may ascend your holy hill? He who has clean hands and a pure heart, who has not lifted his soul to any idol nor spoken what is false, he will ascend into the hill of the Lord, unto the God of his salvation.

Lord God

I am the "Most"

blessed of all men

If I am Humbled without dying!

This is such a Joyous, and Glorious truth Lord!

Please Do it unto Me amen.

Loves theme

My God! If I could take hold of the doors
Of the morning, would I not rend them open
And draw close to you?

If I could take hold of the windows of
Heaven and hold them in my hands, would I
Not rend the heavens open, and leap
Into your arms too?

If I could cry a million oceans of tears
For the lover of my soul, would I not flood
The heavens, in seeking you my God?
For you are my all and my life!

I cry unto you Lord from the depths of my soul,
My heart is hungered after you, come bright and morning star, rend open the
windows of my heart
With the floods of your great love, and take me captive, . . . Willing, . . . Captive,
to the palace of your
House. Do not leave my soul barren for want of you, take me! My heart is
consumed with the
Good theme of your love.

When I look into life's mirror, what there do I see,
Do I see a Man of God there looking back at me? When I look into life's mirror
right into His eyes
Do I see a man of faith there? Or one who lives a lie?
For the just shall live by faith says He and righteousness you know, but do I see
these in my steps as down life's path I go? As I look into life's mirror can I see
the way? Can I see me on the cross, each and every day? Can I see my saviour, as
he dwells in me, or can I see myself, fleeing Calvary? For to live is Christ and to
die is gain,
O death where is your victory
O grave where is your sting?

My bride has long been asleep, and taken many lovers to
her breast; how does she in soiled garments feign before me righteousness?

Prayer without recognition of sin, and true repentance of sin, and sorrow
over the wickedness of our heart, Prayer to our God is but wishful thinking. God
cannot heal a rebellious person, and He will not hear their prayer. We need to
learn from His word, and His Holy Spirit just how wicked we are at heart, in
desire, and attitude, before we can truly repent, and come humbly to Him! Yes as
a man I am writing this, but as much as any other, it applies to me!
God has a time frame, and a time limit for everyone, and everything.
Don't fool around! If you can't hear, if you can't pay attention, if you can't
see, wail and moan, scream and cry out to God! What is it all about God?
Father? What must I do to be saved?
Climb down off of your High horse. You may not know this but your
High horse's name is Pride, which is translated Self, or Me, or even worse,
the proverbial cord of three "not" easily broken: Me, Myself, and I!

This is what we are taught all through life, even in church: Me, Me, Me, Me.
Jesus said you must repent, and be saved from this evil generation!
He also said you must be born again! And give all that you have so that you may
have treasure in Heaven!

My Heart longs and yearns for you Holy Spirit you are true,
My Heart longs, and my desire Holy Spirit for your fire
Living water flow through Me Holy Spirit set me free, free to run down this
Life's
Course Holy Spirit be my source.

Draw me closer Lord to you, let me hear your voice so true
lead me in your holy way Holy Spirit this I pray.

Amen

Bless you Lord Jesus

MUSING
MUSING:——what DO YOU THINK, what is the point of your Life?

Were you put here for a purpose?

Are you simply a biological reproduction of your parents?

Is there a real point to your life?

Where are you going, and for what purpose is it all?

I submit to everyone; You are here for 'No purpose of your own'

God, 'the eternal God either created you strictly for His purpose and eternal Pleasure',

Or, you are here of the worlds natural reproduction, destitute of any salvation, or Real purpose,

And like the brute beasts of the earth simply living until the day you perish and Are no more.

Or a rebellious human whom God would save By Christ Jesus, should you Humble yourself and come to Him.

Now this is not all But it's a lot to Think about. I don't desire to offend, but to Cause you to really think.

I can assure that God Has an eternal purpose for men, and that He made us for His pleasure.

Please read on and see if you can't search Him out.

By the way He is bigger than your biggest opinions! and Does not consider them At all.

He doesn't need your permission for anything, but is willing to save even the worst of sinners like 'me'

My soul so hot within me
my heart will you be still?
My eyes strain from staring
looking, watching for my friend

Oh beloved where must you be
darling pearl of glory draw near

See not that I look to thee, my voice
dos't though not hear?

When my eyes will you find rest
when Jesus face we both posses

When my heart will you be still
when I rest in my Fathers will

When my soul will peace you find
when my master has drawn nigh

Draw niegh unto God and He will
draw nigh unto you

Wash ye in the saviours blood,
and soak in the water of His word

O blessed peace to them that call
upon Him with a pure heart

Those that do His will those that seek
His face and hold up Holy hands

Blessed are they that love His appearing
they seek Him as their treasure

Blessed are they that love His appearing
they are His delight

No hill

There is no hill that I need to climb, no valley to walk through
No rocky waters that I'd like to cross, Lord I just want to be with you

In Spirit and in truth you are, where I want to be
Nothing in this world to want, or do I need to see

My eyes behold you Lord, you are everything to me
That's all there is and nothing more, you are where I want to be

This is not a lamentation, no Lord I would rejoice
For truly I desire to see your Holy face, and to hear your
voice

No mountains left before me now, only one great plain to cross
This world of flesh and blood, to glory in you Lord

Nothing Going On

You say there's nothing going on, nothing fresh and new,
nothing really happening between the Lord and you.
So you go and throw your brain into a world of selfish pleasures,
into a vat of vain pursuits of your own endeavors.
Then you think to come back to Him as His pure and spotless bride.
Not one moment have you stopped to look so deep inside.
Well I don't know about that, think I've got news for you... Jesus knows just
what's inside, and all you say and do. And he's calling us each and every one to
abandon this world of flesh and come, walk in eternity with the Father's Son.
So go and get your heart back from wherever you have sent it and give it back
to Jesus. Find your treasure in His stead, and let the savior fill it then, 'you will
always have something going on something fresh and new.'
Jesus will be in your heart in all you say and do, and when you come to stand before
His holy throne, you will be there happy that you lived for Christ alone. This is the
only thing on earth you really need to know, Take Jesus with you every, everywhere
you go. and your treasure will be in Him, and forever in his kingdom. amen...

What is Idolatry-? Can Christians get it? Is it fatal if they do?
Everything that you do without Christ as your hearts focus.
Idolatry is leaving His kingdom to live in your own.
No not even the worlds, but your own!
Jesus said, I am the way. The truth and the life. And
you must love the Lord with ALL your heart, and soul,
and mind, and strength. If He's got something going on inside of
you, you'll always have a 'testimony' too.

Of God and of Man

If you be reproached for the name of Christ,
Blessed are ye. For the Spirit of glory and of God
Rests upon you. Don't think more highly of yourself
Than you ought to. And don't be weary in well doing.
If your enemy strikes you, offer him the other cheek also.
Don't think to much of yourself, becoming high minded,
But be lowly of heart. So set your mind fully on Jesus Christ
Who is seated close to you, at the right hand of God in the heavenly
Places. Rejoice in the harsh seasons of your life, knowing that
Prosperity and riches are both impostors, and of very little eternal value,
And ought not to be the measure of life. But that true knowledge
Of Jesus Christ is.

Now the test, open book if you like;
Which is of God, and which is of Man?

Oh Canada, our Godforsaken land, unrighteousness runs deep throughout the land, with godless hearts we see the die, corruption ruining all; Gods holy name we take in vain, how long until we fall? God make our land glorious in thee oh Canada we plead to God for thee, oh Canada we plead to God for thee!! Ooh ooh Canada,aa ooh ooh Canada,aa

Oh Canada how sad it is to see the wickedness that's overtaken thee, ungodliness we flaunt and and spread most unashamedly, we do not care for righteousness, oh God how can this be? God make our land glorious in thee, oh Canada we plead to God for thee oh Canada we plead to God for thee! Ooh ooh ooh Canada,aa ooh ooh oh Canada, aa Oh Canada, now people can't you see the wickedness that's overtaken thee? How blind we now as people are when we no longer care, for our only loving God most high, who kindly brought us here? God make our land glorious in thee, oh Canada we plead to God for thee, oh Canada we plead to God for thee! Ooh ooh ooh Canada,aa ooh ooh ooh Canada,aa ooh ooh ooh Canada turn back to G-o-d!!

Oh that we could only see

What is it that I cry out for; In my secret heart of hearts. I hunger and thirst for the precious.
The breath, and the bread of life. You may think me a mad man, 'if I think I am alive you might say'. but I have tasted, and I've seen that Jesus Christ in Me is the only life and way.

How can any man hunger to the edge of utter despair, and then in one sheer cry for help be rescued, and given life so dear? And how can one describe the glory of the King who came to live inside, of those who'd dare to do such a thing as cry out to God? Blessed are those who Hunger and thirst for righteousness; blessed are those who seek the Lord at all times. Blessed are the 'pure' in heart for they shall see God! Oh that Men might see, That men might look hard deep within until they see that God is real.

Oh that I might see that I might see. That I might know as I am truly known.
OH GOD YOU ARE REAL!

Yeah, I'm in the wrong place when, I cannot see your face, When all that lies before me is of the Human race. Cars, and boats, and airplanes. Smoke screens of all kinds. Friendly folks, and neighbours, family so fine. Whatever did you come for Lord, life is just so fine! Fishing, hunting, family, Why do I feel so blind? Something deep within me says throw it all away! I am the truth, I am the life, Son—I am the way!

Long time now I am seeing, that there 'must' be a part, a big piece of eternity that's been missing from my heart. To know you is life my Lord, I know you are the way, yet, I know that I am missing you still this very day! Whatever is this blindness that keeps me in the dark? What ever should I do? And should I run, how far?

Crushed! Yes severely broken, aching, staggering in my heart, I cry to you, I look to you Lord Jesus. how far? Lord how far? Broken, and battered, O my God you are! My heart pants and thirsts for you! Save me! My dear heart.

Truly I waste away, while the wickedest of my enemies say come to me, let's play.

For we sit down to eat, and rise up to play, over, and over, and over again But in my heart I pray Save me Lord from my closest friend, whoever would draw me away.

For a brother is born for adversity, and fun at times is fine, but the Road is hard and treacherous, which leaves this wilderness behind!

You said you want to be real with God! To know His will and ways.
To come into His Kingdom in reality and truth, God says Okay! Ok
But it's gonna hurt! Because if you spent your time entertaining
Your mind, your mind will become a toy rather than a tool.

Lord come, as I sit and wait for you, my heart waits for your Holy touch,
The breath of life is yours to give, and by your Spirit Lord I live.
My mind is reeling from all this pain, my heart burning from all this shame,
My hands defiled with blood and mire, yet my soul is set on you,
You are my one desire! How can I truly come to you? How can I come and be
                                      Renewed?
All manner of snare I've been caught in, and every one of them from sin.
Lord Jesus come and deliver me, cleanse my heart and set my soul and spirit free.
Take my life and draw me near, take my soul and wash it clean.
Come and free me from every snare, The fear of man and this worlds care,
The shame of all of my own sin. Lord I confess, please wash me deep within.
Turn my sickness into health, turn my poverty to wealth, My lack
Father turn to gain, My sin and shame please wash away again.
I pray Jesus in your Holy name, amen.

What in the world is there to gain if I don't have your Spirit?
If I don't have your Spirit I have nothing. Jesus you said "the Spirit is life,
The flesh profits nothing" Lord fill me with your Spirit again and overflow me
With your Holiness I pray in jesus name. amen

The Spirit of God is the beauty of Holiness, the peace of love, and the received Grace For eternal life in Jesus Christ. The presence of the Person, the Holy Spirit giving Comfort to a wounded soul, for the spirit is life the flesh profits nothing! Blessed Be His Holy name.

The day of the Lord

When the day of the Lord comes, where will His Majesty find 'you?'
One thing I ask Lord, that will I seek, that I may dwell in the house of the Lord,
To behold the beauty of the Lord and to enquire in His temple.
It is a fearful thing to fall into the hands of the living God. But far better to fall
Into
The hands of the living God in sheer terror of Him, than to not fall into His
Hands
Until the last day. There is no other place for me! I want with all my heart to
Fall into His hands today, to face His judgment today, while I may be able to
Repent rather than to risk being
Puffed up with myself in pride risking His eternal judgment on that day when
It's too late!

We have no common ground with God until we are crucified with Christ. For
flesh cannot enter the kingdom of God. Therefore we must put off the deeds of
the flesh, and all of its desires, being dead to the flesh and alive to God Dead to
the world and alive to Christ, For the scripture says, For you Have died and your
life is hidden with Christ in God. Therefore it is no longer I who live, but Christ
who lives within me. Jesus come! Lord Jesus come! Have mercy on your people,
who claim you, but don't know you. Save those who seek your Kingdom with
intensity, and purpose, to truly know you God!

Covered

You are covered in My blood. Yes, the mighty cleansing flood.
No, not worldly wisdom, small, My blood is great, and all in all.
Powerful to make one whole, to wash and heal you once for all.
My chosen vessels will contain, all I shed to bring them in.
Every drop has paid the cost, none of My precious blood was lost!
Now it covers head to toe, My beloved whom I know.
They'll be with Me one day soon, you can know this, this is true.
How they ache for Me to come. How unto My presence run,
Seeking precious time with Me, how they hunger just to see.
One thing they ask, yes, this they seek, to behold My beauty, and to speak.
No other wonder, no none at all, will they seek, they will not call.
These are mine, with a true heart, they are small and set apart,
My eye is steadfast upon them, I'll not turn away from them.

ONE THING,

Are You Saved?

Are you saved don't look at me,

Don't look at your neighbour, brother, sister or anyone else.

Don't even look at some small child, or new born babe . . .

Look at you are you saved?

If you died today, If you died tonight, would you
Go to be with Jesus Christ or would you go to hell?

Are you saved?

Satan has an agenda, to deflect you away from this grilling question until its to late.

His greatest tool which has worked wonders is to get men and women to look
At anyone, anything other than their own hearts. because while you question
Another you are not likely to look at you

Are you I do mean 'you' saved?

What does God mean to you? do you hunger for His kingdom, for His Spirit, for Holiness in you?
Can you say Jesus come! come Lord! Or do you say something 'anything' else?

Are you 'you know' saved?

Options?

There are no options on the cross. Everything you thought
You'd gained, now you see was really loss!
The ones that you called lovers, and friend, are the ones who nailed you
There. You now are cast upon the altar, not one worldly care!
It's shameful now that you can see the things that kept you from this
Glory tree; No other thing could ere compare with the glory of dying
Here, on your own tree, dying to yourself, at your own Gethsemane;
Oh the glory to appear, apart from you, Christ so near! Wonder, and
Majesty now enthroned, His grace on you, yes you alone!
Heaven to bear . . .

Psalm 19 on my mind

The Heavens declare the Glory of God; and the firmament shows His handiwork. Day unto day utters speech, and night unto night reveals knowledge. There is no speech nor language where their voice is not heard. Their line has gone out through all the earth, and their words to the end of the world. In them He has set a tabernacle for the sun, which is like a bridegroom coming out of His chamber, and rejoices like a strong man to run it's race. It's rising is from one end of the Heaven, and it's circuit is to the other; And there is nothing Hidden from it's heat. The law of the Lord is perfect, converting the soul; the testimony of the Lord is sure, making wise the simple; The statutes of the Lord are right rejoicing the Heart; The commandment of the Lord is pure, enlightening the eyes; The fear of the Lord is clean, enduring forever. The judgments of the Lord are true and righteous altogether. More to be desired are they than Gold, yea, much fine Gold; Sweeter also than honey and the honeycomb. Moreover by them your servant is warned, and in keeping them there is great reward.

Who can understand his errors? Cleanse me from my secret faults. Keep back your servant also from presumptuous sins; Let them not have dominion over me. Then I shall be blameless, and I shall be innocent of great transgression. Let the words of my mouth and the meditation of my Heart Be acceptable in your sight, O Lord my strength and my redeemer.

Psalm 38
A Psalm of David. To bring to remembrance.

O LORD, do not rebuke me in Your wrath,
Nor chasten me in Your hot displeasure!
For Your arrows pierce me deeply,
And Your hand presses me down.

There is no soundness in my flesh
Because of Your anger,
Nor any health in my bones
Because of my sin.
For my iniquities have gone over my head;
Like a heavy burden they are too heavy for me.
My wounds are foul and festering
Because of my foolishness.

I am troubled, I am bowed down greatly;
I go mourning all the day long.
For my loins are full of inflammation,
And there is no soundness in my flesh.
I am feeble and severely broken;
I groan because of the turmoil of my heart.

Lord, all my desire is before You;
And my sighing is not hidden from You.
My heart pants, my strength fails me;
As for the light of my eyes, it also has gone from me.

My loved ones and my friends stand aloof from my plague,
And my relatives stand afar off.
Those also who seek my life lay snares for me;
Those who seek my hurt speak of destruction,
And plan deception all the day long.

But I, like a deaf man, do not hear;
And I am like a mute who does not open his mouth.
Thus I am like a man who does not hear,
And in whose mouth is no response.

For in You, O LORD, I hope;
You will hear, O Lord my God.
For I said, "Hear me, lest they rejoice over me,
Lest, when my foot slips, they exalt themselves against me."

For I am ready to fall,
And my sorrow is continually before me.
For I will declare my iniquity;
I will be in anguish over my sin.
But my enemies are vigorous, and they are strong;
And those who hate me wrongfully have multiplied.
Those also who render evil for good,
They are my adversaries, because I follow what is good.

Do not forsake me, O LORD;
O my God, be not far from me!
Make haste to help me,
O Lord, my salvation!

Quiet

Quiet; Its so quiet, I thought I heard an angle cry.
I thought I saw within My heart, as with his wings He
Hid His eyes. Crying Holy! Holy! Holy! Then faded off
Into the sacred silence of his own place.

Sitting down I took my pen to capture such a sight,
My heart reeling, tearing, and moved to tears, as deep within I cry Holy, Holy,
Holy! And I drift off into a quit,
Silent sigh.

Blessed are you Lord, Blessed is Your Holy name.
amen

Quirky quote? free for all!
Shepherds should never mend their
fences with sheep skin!

Better it is to stretch yourself over a
rift, through a breach, or across a chasm,
than to drag a wounded lamb across the
wasteland of your own pride . . . .

*Remember the Lord,
remember the Lord! Son rest your hope fully on the grace that will be revealed to
you at the revelation of Jesus Christ. Hope and Glory only in Him, even in His Holy
name! You will not fall that my righteous right arm will not reach out and catch
you Son. I know your ways, even of late, and that you hate your own sin and are
ashamed of it. I will yet thoroughly change you, save you and transform you into
the image of Jesus Christ, you must again strive to enter the narrow gate, which
is difficult, and Hard, and remember that the road to destruction, is real, popular,
fun, and easy and there are many who travel it. But because the road that leads to
eternal life, joy, and Glory is rocky, rough, harsh at times, and hard there are few
that find, or desire it.*

Rend your Hearts

Rend your heart, and not your garments; pretend ye not at all;
Let your heart be broken open, let your 'self' be crushed and fall;
Break that will that's all about you, cast it to the ground and call,
Crying out to Abba Father, free me Lord from all; My all;
Rend your heart, and toss it from you; throw it very far;
For like mine it is deceitful, and it has been from the start.
Don't you look into your mirror, to make yourself seem fair,
You will find the truthful answer if you linger there!
Look instead, and listen closely to God's Holy word;
See your life as vain and shallow, then come running to the Lord.
"I am God" and you are nothing! Yes, I know that Lord.
I wish I were something, just enough, to speak to you one word!?
Then, to Hear you as truly as I am heard . . .

I love you Jesus

Rest your hope fully on the grace that shall be 'given' to
You at the revelation of Jesus Christ.

C'mon, C'mon, listen closely sons and daughters, brothers, and sisters
Mothers, and Fathers!

I came to Give you life! C'mon, don't hold back any more!
Nothing in this world is worth it!

I have called you friend. You say to Me, Brother, But when you are at home
Again, your love is another! Your Heart is closed, and fat as grease, your Holy
Passion
Now has ceased. You cling to another, Mother, daughter, sister, brother!

I am the way, I am the life, I am the all in all. I have come to call, to Me my wife
I have come for one and all, who truly take my name, and not in vain. Not in
pretence,
or for sordid gain. I am the treasure of every life. If you are mine you are my
wife, and you love me, you love me true, I have come, I've come for you.

Set aside your lovers, the ones there with you, set aside, set aside your
Pleasures come and be my darling bride.

Cast on me your every care, I am your life now if you are mine,
You now have eternal life, that is, life divine.

Don't you understand this? Don't you even see, you were dead
I gave you life, now should you live just for Me!

When will you Hear?

Scripture says From the rising of the sun till the going down of the same, The name of the Lord is to be praised!

And who can know this Lord? the one who created the heavens and the Earth? the one who declares a thing and it is done?

Who can know such a God as this, a God who has Eyes that see and ears that hear? A God who dwells in unapproachable light, Who bows Himself to look upon the Earth?

He who has clean hands and a pure heart, who has not lifted up his soul to any idol, nor speaks what is false, He who has a broken heart, and a contrite spirit. This is the man that the Lord draws near to Him, giving the such a one eyes that see and ears that do hear. My friends please draw near to this God with all your heart.

Do you realize that God does not care what you think, or of your opinion on anything at all? He only looks to see if there is anyone who will humble themselves and confess that He is God of all and saves such as are lowly of heart.

Lord Jesus praise be to your Holy name amen. save your people Lord.

Repent and Believe

Repent and believe. Repent and be converted. Repent and be baptized. He who believes will be saved. Those who believe and are baptized will be saved.

Come out from among them, be separate. And I shall be your God and you shall be my people. This people Honor me with their lips but their Heart is far from Me. Go into the entire world and preach. And make disciples. These signs will follow those who believe. They will cast out Demons They will speak with new tongues. they will take up serpents and they will not harm them.

Jesus laid it all down straight. If you abide in My word, and My word abides in you, My Father and I will abide in you. He who comes to God must believe that He is and that He is the rewarder of those who diligently seek Him. I am your exceeding great reward {He says}

Because abiding in Christ, and Christ abiding in you is the 'ONLY' reward that is eternal, and the only reward that is worth anything. My crown of glory, and my pearl of greatest price is Christ 'in Me' [the hope of glory]. Christ in Me, He is my all, in all. Christ in Me [He is the life] Christ in me from glory to glory, to the fullness of the stature of the measure of Christ. And if I have eyes that see, and ears that hear, and the body rejects the eyes, then the eyes are alone, and are helpless, and the body is left blind. Christ in you is the only hope of glory. Paul said for if, for this life only we have faith we are of all people the most pity-able! This people sit down to eat, and rise up to play. My house shall be a house of prayer. [I am the exceeding great reward] If you abide in My words; If anyone loves Me he will keep my words, And we will come to Him and make our home with Him. But the helper the Holy Spirit, whom the Father will send in my name. He will teach you all things, and bring to your remembrance all things that I said to you.

Lord give us ears that really hear I pray amen.

Seek ye first

*Seek ye first as you Have sought, as you would grasp
the edge, those whom you loved and trusted saw it
as their duty in Christ, or in themselves, to tear from
your High calling, which is the same for them. Seek
ye first the Kingdom, they continued to pull you down,
not that you were exalting yourself, but my kingdom
to come, so you went away and got weary of doing
well and suddenly satan threw you a snare, and suddenly
you fell, I am glad that you've hit the bottom, for I can
reach you there. I always knew where to find you,
I always heard you prayer. Now don't you fret or worry
many are the called, but few are chosen, from those
who make another fall. I am here, and right beside you,
I have seen your ways, I gently say repent my son and
I'll direct you paths and days . . .*

Seed or nut

Jesus told his disciples; unless a man forsake
all that He has he cannot be my disciple.
He also said unless a seed falls to the ground and dies it is by itself,
but if it fall to the ground and dies it will spring up and produce a harvest.
My thought for us this morning is; are we His seed? Are we losing everything of
the world for His sake?
or are we 'Nuts' desperately clinging to the branches' of this world so as to preserve
our lives?
Jesus said whoever tries to save his life would lose it, but whoever loses His life for
His sake and the gospels sake would find it.
Lord grant us repentance that we might let go of this world and fall onto your
Holy ground, amen.

Shadowed road

I walked along a shadowed road
The shadow was despair, I drug along this
Heavy load, taking everywhere.

I never knew there was a life apart from
Such a pain, until I found the cross of Christ, and
That He rose again.

I entered to Gethsemane and I bowed down to pray
Rose up and took my cup and turned to walk away
I thought I live in Gethsemane, and as I went to go
I knew I had to drink this cup, my cup was from the lord.

Through many trials and tests, the way we enter in
And through a broken heart the way is made within
So I drink this cup My Father has prepared, and one day
Filled with fresh new wine I'll drink it at home with Him.

Son give me your year

For we must all appear before the Judgement seat Christ, that each one may the things done in the body, according to what he has done whether good or bad.

—Knowing therefore the terror of the Lord, we persuade men.

I stood there at my post, and watched the day go by. A sentry so I thought, as I sat and time passed nigh . . . then suddenly, I startled, as the King stood and spoke to me; suddenly in terror, my ears could not perceive!

Servant give to me your year! My heart smashed, and it smote me.

I could give no account. I was to be an honoured servant, but I'd revelled at sins fount! My sin, I not ashamed of till this moment. So shamed me, while His glory stood before of me. The blood in my head truly pounding, I thought I'd lose my sight, the past full year of sinfulness flashing fiercely before my eyes!

Screaming out, I cried aloud for mercy from my Lord, not a sound perceptible,

no word came from my voice. I knew that only evil was the truth of everything I'd done, And instantly before His Holiness was broken and undone.

Called as seed for holiness, living such a ruse. 'I' inward then crumbling, for evil no excuse!
Give me your year! Again I heard, this is your day of truth!
Your post shall soon be removed, ere you come forth reproved!
Still I cannot answer! You have seen it all! I the chief of sinners.
This no doubt, no doubt at all . . . not one second can I bring; not one pure and

Holy thing

my garment of the year is stained with the blood of many many sin.
How can I retain my post, my place with you O Lord of Hosts?

What can I ere think to bear before my mighty King?
O Lord only this of a heart of simplicity and of devotion to thee.
For Christ in me, is my only mercy hope of glory. Now again Lord may I see,

Please deliver me

Please deliver me—from all that I can be without you.

Please deliver me, from the treasures of this world, without you.

Take away the trappings of wealth and of pleasure, and the fullness of life that are in the flesh

Please deliver me from what so many people—call being blessed.

I don't need to zoom across the waters in a big old fancy boat, I'd rather walk on rocky waters with you Jesus my Lord. Please deliver me.

Please deliver me from Harley Davidson, from Chevrolet and GMC and all the other wonders of men. Please deliver me from the internet, from Microsoft and Bill Gates, And all the things I haven't said yet! Please Lord deliver Me from all the lust that my eyes can see, please Lord deliver me from my own flesh, arise up in me by your Spirit.

Please deliver me from all I cannot see, from the hope that poverty puts on me to be rich, and free. All the snares and lies of men who have glory in all the riches and alibi's they use to spite and spurn thee.
Please deliver me, from all my fears and pain, from all the hopeless shame that has come over me, come and hold my hand, come and hold me close to thee, let me put my head upon your breast Lord deliver me. Let me put my head upon your breast Lord Deliver me . . .

Stand up

Stand up! Don't you cower in the trenches, we're in a different kind of war.
So get out in the open, let them shoot at you some more!
The battle lines have all been drawn, No coward ever will march on,
The shooting will go on and on, until the victory of the Cross is won.

Your helmet, it is bullet proof, nothing that the foe can do,
Though he wrestles hard, and twists you sore,
The victory belongs to Jesus Christ, the battle is the Lord's!

The trench is like a ditch, not a place to hide.
It's also like a rut, no place for a perfect bride!
When were hiding there, no wounds we think we'll take,
But being hidden in the dark, is Satan's perfect ruse, and rake.

So let us come out in the open, let us stand up clean and pure,
Let Jesus Christ shine bright upon us, and take some shots for Him for sure.
When we stand for Christ our rock, no more cheap, and shallow talk,
Satan will attack for sure, But we'll surly have the victory for the battle is the
Lords.

Isaiah says; No weapon formed against us shall prosper, and every tongue
That rises up against us we shall condemn.

Supply

*Now He who supplies the Spirit to you and works miracles
among you, does He do it by works of the law, or by hearing of faith? Gal 3:5*

*Now how is it that men may know the Lord, the God of all creation? How is it
that He may supply the power to do miracles, Yes even to Men, Common men? How
is it that a former blasphemer, or Idolatrous man may ever perform even one Holy
miracle? By what name, or what Spirit? How?*

*First He must enter the Holy, of Holies! All the gifts, and the calling of God come
through the Holy, of Holies, Through any vessel that the Lord chooses to bring there.
That is the Holy presence of the Holy God, Yahweh! There is No other!*

*Hebrews 11:6 Those who come to God, Must believe that He is and that He is a
rewarder of those who diligently seek Him. God is the reward for those who diligently
seek Him. Truly, truly in all the earth and in all creation there is absolutely No other
reward at all! So when a man comes to God, diligently seeking Him, and finds Him,
That man will die in His presence, He will cease to exist. For when one comes so
close to God, He is born again, the old man has passed away and God has created
a new creature in Christ Jesus! yes He really is a brand new person, who now has
an awe-ful, and awesome Father! Abba! Now since He has this new Dad He has
access to all of His Dads stuff. Not only that, now he posses His dads attributes,
even His nature.*

*Can any man therefore do these signs and wonders? Yes! Emphatically Yes, for God
is Not a respecter of persons. So then How? By the Same Holy Spirit that raised
Jesus Christ from the dead.*

How? Those who 'come' to God, not to church, not to pastor Sofine, Not to

*Any man. Those who come to God! Do you know that it is God who puts in men the
ability, the authority, the Spirit, the everything, both to will and to work for His good
pleasure? I'm pretty sure that most pastors would secretly if not outwardly be very
upset if all the Gifts of God suddenly started to happen in all of their churches.*

*Because their one man shows would be set aside for full body function, and power.
Which is the Kingdom call, and command!*

Then to the witness of the power of God would be evident. With healing, conversions, and many new births, with Much rejoicing in Spirit and in truth.

Would to God that His Holy FIRE were kindled in every house!
And that men everywhere would lift up Holy hands without wrath, or doubting, and I say fervently pursue the face of Christ. Man if we only knew Him!

The Attitudes

Blessed are the poor in Spirit, for theirs is the Kingdom of God.

Blessed are those who mourn, for they shall be comforted.

Blessed are the meek, for they shall inherit the earth.

Blessed are those who hunger and thirst for righteousness, for they shall be filled.

Blessed are the merciful, for they shall obtain mercy.

Blessed are the pure in heart, for they shall see God.

Blessed are those who are persecuted for righteousness sake, for theirs is the Kingdom of Heaven.

Blessed are you when they revile and persecute you, and say all kinds of evil against you 'falsely' for my sake.

Rejoice and be exceedingly glad, for great is your reward in Heaven.

Who is blind but my servant, or deaf as my messenger whom I send?

Seeing many things, but you do not observe; Opening the ears but he does not Hear?

Ok.—Okay here's the test. Here's the window in the wall, the door of the house.

Are you Ready, are you Really ready?

Dig deep on this one, it's not obvious. Hang on tight; it might take a day or two.

Are You Blessed?

The acceptable

When Jesus Christ truly becomes the pearl of greatest price to His body the church, 'today' will be the acceptable day of the Lord. And the Spirit, And the Bride will Cry come! Come Lord Jesus, Come bright and morning star, Oh Lord come. Jesus came to us as the anointed only begotten of the Father, He came to pay the demand of God, blood for Sin. His pure blood was the only blood ever that could pay the price. He came to set the captives free, He came to give life, and that More abundantly, He came to give everlasting life to all who would come to Him with a broken heart and a contrite spirit. He came to heal every disease and to make many Disciples, He came and preached the acceptable year of the Lord, and the vengeance of our God. He said when you pray, pray in this manner; Our Father which art in Heaven Hallowed be thy name. Thy Kingdom come, Thy will be done, on Earth as in Heaven; Give us this day our daily bread, and forgive our trespasses as we forgive those who trespass against us an lead us not into temptation but deliver us from the evil one. Yes, Lord come! The acceptable year of the Lord.

The Feather

There's a feather in your hat, oh man!—That feather is your pride!
For you have hunted and taken trophies—My treasure is my bride.
She is spotless, pure, and holy—Completely without stain.
Yet you look for other trophies—To tag to your own name!
Your feathers, horns, and trinkets—The idols that you love.
They all are separators—To keep you from the Lord our God.
Why do you not see this?—I will truly say
You do not see the truth—The life, the light, the way
I AM!

The stone of which you builders—So easily cast away
It is the only stone—That any man can lay
It is the stone of repentance—From deep within every heart
To be saved from this generation—Forever to depart!
It is the rock of ages—To truly be the bride
Of Jesus Christ the Saviour—Being crucified
No more witty wonder words—No more songs of fools
No more jingle jangle—No more golden rules
Only come to Jesus—Lay down your life and pride
Climb upon His altar—Be a living sacrifice!
"To the cross with you," I cry!—There to bear Him evermore
To be bound and chained to Him—Prisoner of the Lord
There is no greater honor—Than to be crucified with Christ
Born of the new baptism—A willing sacrifice

The Glory of God

How great is the Glory of God? How great is the Glory of God! How awesome is the one who spoke, and the universe was created! Yes the world and all it contains! God touches the mountains and they Smoke. God's voice shakes the Heaven's and the Earth. He shakes the world and everything in it. To shake out those things that cannot remain, {because they are not His} so that the things that are His may remain. {Hebrews 12-27}

He shook the Earth when He saved Noah, and his family, Killing, everyone else with a global flood. I wonder does that make him seem evil to you. Better not, that proves He is just, and holy, and that He hates evil. What would you have done, being pure, just, and holy, filled with majestic glory? See, because you are not, you cannot see why or how God could do that.

Do you know Him, He says to know Him is life. He said that the anti-diluvian [pre flood] world was totally corrupt, and that the thoughts of their heart was on violence continually. He said he made man upright, but they sought out many schemes. Where do you stand, can you handle His glory? We shall see! You would say, the day is glorious, or the sunshine is glorious, or the weather, or old age, or children, or grand children. But God made these things merely speaking them into being! Listen, if a million or so earths would fit into the sun, and a hundred million suns would fit into Canis majoris, say it would take man a zillion light years to traverse our known universe, {God's spoken sentence} Uni—single verse–sentence. Also considering that light travels at the speed of one hundred and eighty six thousand miles per second. How can you imagine yourself able to be near Him, or in His presence? His glory, He says He will share with no man! One obvious reason after considering these things is, No human can. They would completely implode, or explode or something! He says that no flesh will glory in His presence.

Listen if we could begin to conceive, or begin to comprehend who God is! Wow. Our first response would be to us an earth shattering silence! As we for the first time learn what terror is. And what the fear of the Lord is. And what it means to be humble, as humble as a nonexistent thing.—We would first find that shutting up is the best thing that we could ever do! Then in our first time quiet—we would hear God's voice, as it shatters rocks and shakes mountains. That still small voice which is louder than all the echoes of His glorious creation. The Lord! He is God! Scripture says 'no man can look upon God and live'. He will share His glory with no man.—{no man could take it} No man could survive it.

Men are completely rebellious to God and we cannot even see this until we realize how Glorious He is, and how proud, and arrogant we are! // O Man! Father God We really need you to show us your glory. Father, shake us awake, I ask Father that you shake me until I wake up, until Christ Jesus shines on me. Thy kingdom come in me, thy will be done as well In Jesus Christ holy name!! Amen.

All the wisdom of men, of science, and societies is less than nothing to you God, Less than nothing. The only ones who can perceive these things are the humble, who seek you with the whole heart. Answer me speedily oh Lord, my Spirit fails; do not hide your face from me lest I be like those who go down to the Pit. Cause me to hear you loving kindness in the morning for I trust in you, teach me the way in which I should walk for unto you I lift up my soul. Lord you are in Heaven, and I am on earth, therefore I am devoted to fearing you.

Lord all I have ever done before you is sin. It amazes me to no end, how so many people, 'see themselves' as 'good' man, there is no such creature. Scripture in Romans say 'for all have sinned, and fallen short of the glory of God! It could say that, all they've ever done is sin! Jesus said why do you call me good, 'no one is good', except God.

Here we go again. Try to come close to glorying in 'you' as you ponder these things. Try to bring your stuff close to God. In your pride, present Him your life; show Him your family, your house, whatever you want. Then tell Him how wonderful it all is, how glorious your children are. You don't know who you are talking to. By now some will think, yes but God is an all merciful God! Yes He is. But you cannot know His mercy, before you know His Glory! Glory precedes mercy because if it were the other way, men would never come to know him. Nor would you really know His mercy. If we don't understand how staggering, and stunning He is in His glory, we could never understand how desperately we need His stunning, and staggering Mercy, and at best all we could be before Him is a pretender, or lukewarm. Deceivers and false teachers try to bring to you a shallow Gospel, where nothing happens to you, except that you say, 'you believe'. Scripture's say the demons believe as well, but they shudder. They are terrified of God.—Still they continue in their ways, because they are demons. Why do we continue to mock God, and continue to live for our flesh, and for pleasure? Jesus said 'unless your righteousness exceeds the righteousness of the scribes and the Pharisees, you will not enter the kingdom of God. Was He lowering God's standard here or raising it? These men were very religious, very strict, but they didn't know the Lord in Spirit and in truth! They followed rules, but holiness was far from their Heart. Hebrews says, Without Holiness no one shall see the Lord. {Who are you Lord, Apostle Paul cried out, on the road to Damascus}

His, traditions of the Fathers, His ignorant zeal for His family, or familiar way was shattered, and for three days He was left blind. The Glory of the Lord had fallen upon Him. The light of God's glory, so strong that Paul, a zealous man was struck blind—Where are you? In relation to such a one as Christ, where do you stand, Jesus said once, pray that you may be able to stand before the son of man. Lord I repent! Lord I tear out my own heart. Please save Me! A wicked man. Jesus said the gate is narrow, and difficult is the way. In the Bible the people would tear their clothes in anguish when they saw the Holiness of God, and their sinfulness. The prophet Joel came along and said, Tear your hearts, and not your garments, probably because tearing their clothes became a show, or a performance, and was not real, heartfelt repentance. It's kind of like the woman who conceives, and brings forth a bunch of children, all from different men. Then she tries to convince her husband that they are all his. Then as they grow up, and become who they really are, they do not act like, or look like, or think the husband, because the children, will be as their fathers were. [The scripture's say the seed is in the father.] You can find a parallel to this in Hosea. What kind of offspring are you? All of this woman's offspring were illegitimate. Not one of them was the husbands. How could they stand with Him? They were completely different. How can illegitimate {not His} humans stand with a holy God? Jesus condemned sectarianism, yet we have something like thirty eight thousand different denominations in the world. How many of the harlots children are there, how many illegitimate sons and daughters are there? How can any reflect the Father when they are not His?

Are you getting any of this? Paul said Christ came to save sinners of which I am Chief! The Harlot mother says these children are all God's children! What. Jesus said to the religious leaders Satan is your father, and His desire you always seek to do! If she was God's, and her children were God's her confession would be like Paul's I am the greatest of sinners. 'All I have ever done is sin', but now they call evil good, and good they call evil. So now bring these ones close to God, let them share His glory; do you see that this is imposable? Their glory is in their shame. Lord help us to wake up! Help us to repent as Paul did. I used to pray Father, make me blind to the things of this world, so that I can see the things of God! There is Mercy for sin. There is ample mercy for sin. There is ample forgiveness. But not without "real" recognition of wickedness, and bone marrow deep acknowledgment of it before the Lord God. Will you come and glory in your sin before God? Not at all.

He says a broken heart, and a contrite Spirit He will not deny. He won't turn away a repentant Heart. I have probably done as much evil as anyone, but I didn't try to fool God, and bring my evil to Him in self deception, I really confessed it as evil in His sight!

"What does this offend you?"
"What does this offend you". Remember when Jesus said this in John 6:62? What does this offend you, what if you should see the son of man ascend where He was before? 6:63 it is the Spirit that gives life the flesh profits nothing. The words that I speak to you, they are life. But there are some of you who do not believe; therefore I have said to you that no one can come to me unless it has been granted to Him by my Father.

Verse 6:66 Then scripture says, Form that time many of His disciples went back and walked with Him no more. Then Jesus said to the twelve, do you want to go away also? Peter said: to whom shall we go? You have the words of life, also we have come to believe and know that you are the Christ the Son of God. Jesus answered them, did I not choose you the twelve, and one of you is a Devil? Oh man is anybody getting this?

O man is anybody getting this?

In John 6:66 we see that the Disciples had reached their limit. They had followed Jesus, were fed by Jesus, they were healed by Him, in everything natural they rejoiced. But when it came time to go deep into the eternal, everlasting, supernatural, the Kingdom of God and everlasting life through the blood of Jesus Christ, the blood of the Lamb of God, No way could they take that! But Jesus said, unless you eat of my flesh, and drink of my blood, you have no life in you. Whoever eats of my flesh and drinks of my blood has eternal life, and I will raise Him up on the last day.

Something changed! Now those who followed for pleasure, enjoyment, a show, and food, even healing, had to do something. {Feed on the word of God} Christianity was never meant to be a culture, or a club, But a complete life changing, and transforming, totally encompassing eternal event, for all who believe. Who believe in Spirit and in truth. He is the bread of life, and all who truly come to Him, delight in dinning on Him. Feasting at the table, on His bread, and drinking the wine, the blood of His everlasting promise, {life}! I praise you Lord! I praise you Jesus. From everlasting to everlasting you are God! It is the Glory of God to conceal a thing. It is the Glory of kings to search it out! Dig deep into the wells of salvation.
Who will ascend God's holy Mountain, who will abide in His presence? The ones who delight in fresh bread, the living bread, the word of God. The word of God is their food. The Holy Ghost is their teacher. They Delight in Yeshua, Jesus Christ. How big is God? Think of this, what if our biggest star Canis Majoris were to come right up close to the earth, like fifty feet away { that would wreck everybody on earth! } Forget about gravity, or magnetic pull and all that. Just this massive Star 'right there' fifty feet away from 'you'. All you could see would be this star. You couldn't see anything else anywhere. And suddenly your brain would be upside down, and down would be up, and up would be down, and because its size and closeness you would think that you surely will fall onto it.

By the way likely what you just envisioned is something about earth's size, maybe about eight thousand miles diameter. Canis Majoris would be a million or more times that size. And, Our God spoke them both into being. Where can you stand next to Him? He is terrifying! Just terrifying! Apostle Paul said {knowing the terror of the Lord we persuade men!} And In Hebrews it says in one place it is a terrible thing to fall in to the hands of the living God. Where then will you stand? How glorious is our God!?
He is so pure that He could sit forever on His throne, and Never have to speak a word. He is so pure that as we sit, be still and know that He is God, we are

crushed by the weight of His purity, and while we are being crushed we know——I am such a dog--. How pure, how glorious, how magnificent is our God. That in Him we live, and move and have our being. In Him we live. We could not live if He didn't give the things of life, just to mention one, {the air we breathe} Consider the universe again scientists say that this planet is the only place out there with an atmosphere, and life sustaining components. This is the only place with oxygen, and all living creatures need oxygen to live. In Him we move, and have our being. Peter says in Scripture. With the Lord one day is as a thousand years, and a thousand years is as one day. God is timeless and constant. He spoke all things into existence. Our being is a direct result of His speaking his creation into being. {Not our sin, and the evil we have done} For since Adam sinned, everything went away from God's original plan. The world rebelled. So we now look not to the original plan {in the beginning} But we look to the Call, the upward calling of God in Christ Jesus. For God was in the world reconciling the world to himself, and he has given to us this ministry of reconciliation. Here is a millennia of understanding. Caution here, How can you be reconciled to one you never knew?

Those who come to God 'must' believe that He is and that He is the rewarder of those who diligently seek Him. Let me tell you here, God is the reward of those who diligently seek Him. {He says, I am your exceeding, great reward.} Earnestly, tenderly Jesus is calling, calling for you and for me, come Home, come home, ye who are weary come Home; I do not make an emotional, impassioned plea here, no. Jesus said Repent, and be converted! Be changed! Be born again! Behold I have come to give you life, and that more abundantly! Not flesh life, but everlasting life. He is the life.

You say I can stand by God; I am as good as anyone else. You also are as bad as anyone else. Pride, I {eye} problems, begin with pride. Pride causes men to become the centre of their own lives. Humility causes them to repent, and to come to God. No flesh can glory in His presence. Can you stand before an earthly King? Can you run up and down His aisles? Then how can you stand before the Lord of Hosts, the maker of the universe, which we cannot begin to comprehend?

Aside. Ephasians says that we shall be judged for every Idle word we speak.

Still God loves to hear us speak. He loves our voices. He loves language. Nowhere in the all of the universe is there language, or speech other than here on earth, and in heaven. The very thought of the exclusivity of speech between Men and God should cause us to fear before Him. If only we could figure out whom we are talking to, when we are talking to God.

Father, please crush me, that I might be a broken and contrite vessel before you, that you may use my life to touch, and reach others for you glory.

I pray for a deeper understanding of you, and your eternal kingdom for everyone whom reads these words, and for myself as well. Lord please show us you're Glory In Jesus Christ amen.

The Lord's Warrior I

Hands clasped together, gripping tightly to the handle of His weapon, the warrior steps forth from the glaring brightness of the day, and walks confidently off into the darkness, the deep darkness of the night. There is a fierce resolve in His eyes, so fierce that you almost cannot bear to look into them. But even with the cutting, piercing, fierceness you can perceive the 'purity' and the gentleness of the Heart beneath. 'The Lord's Warrior'. His sword gleams in the darkness and the light of it burns and reveals the hearts of men. He has a helmet upon his head, the saving grace of the glorious master, the helmet that declares without a word, Salvation is of the Lord, and of the Kingdom of our God. On His feet He wears the shoes of Peace, Melchizedek, King of righteousness, King of peace.
On His loins, the belt of truth, Our God reigns, every knee shall
bow, and every tongue confess that Jesus Christ is Lord! Upon His chest He wears the breastplate of the righteousness of Christ, as He wields the shield of faith to extinguish every fiery dart of the enemy. He raises His sword in His right hand, and His open palm, His left, and roars a mighty roar of Honour, and Worship; Blessed are you O God, Blessed is the God of all Creation! Glory to your name my Father! I praise you, I magnify your Holy name. I glorify you my God. I glory in your Holy name Jesus, Yeshua.

Steadfastly He declares, you who have begun a good work in
Me, will complete it until the day of Christ Jesus, the day of your coming. Nevertheless, come Lord Jesus come, the Spirit and the bride say come!

He steps forth, He clasps His hands to the horns of the altar of incense, again he roars a mighty roar from deep within His being, ABBA, Father! . . . . Thy Kingdom is an Everlasting Kingdom
Thy word O God is truth! Your righteousness is like the mighty mountains, and I put my trust in you! Thy Kingdom come Father. Thy will be done Oh my Master! You are my Father.

I extol you my God and I praise you! Father I bless your Holy name.
As He praises and continues to pray, 'voice shaking', hands fiercely
gripping to the horns of the altar, His roar of Honour and Praise
Turns to groaning, groaning too deep for words. His knees begin to buckle from the weight of the burden He bears. And now on His face, the groans turn to convulsions of deep groaning intercession, tapering off to silent sobs pleading for the desire of His heart. In a whisper now, His heart cries 'Come Lord Jesus, the Spirit and the

bride say come. O Yeshua my redeemer come; my heart longs for you. I long for your presence, my Lord, Come!'

When He arises He returns to take hold of the Horns of the Golden altar, and confesses 'Lord I am so honoured to be your child. I bless your Holy name. I ask for your presence in power in my land by the blood of Jesus Christ. Power to save! Turn my people unto you Lord, bring Glory to your Holy name, throughout this land, Lord I pray.'

He traverses celestial boundaries, ascending to the heavens of God! He is neither hot nor cold, yet the vastness of the universal space seems endless! As He travels there, He senses the presence of some other being, a foul presence of evil; Still the cry of His heart and the call of His soul are fixed upon the object of His love, the very reason and purpose of His sojourn! Once again the accuser is there, who night and day stands accusing the brethren. The warrior stands, resisting His adversary until they are in the presence of the Lord of Hosts! The warrior, steadfast in faith resists, As they approach the throne room of God, the warrior's Heart grows with love, and reverence, Holy love with Fear! He comes before the Father of Lights, to the Right hand of the Majesty on High. He comes, and now He bows his knees, both to the Father, and unto the Lamb, in all Fear and Holy reverence. Again he confesses 'Jesus, you are everything to me. I bow to You!'

The accuser also there, begins to accuse violently and wildly, with great arrogance and pride! As the warrior child of God continues in His lowly submission, until the Ancient of Days proclaims: "The Lord rebuke you Satan! Who shall bring a charge against God's elect? It is God who justifies! Who is He who condemns? It is Christ who died and furthermore is also risen!"Who is even at the right hand of God! With His stern rebuke the Devil flees the Holy presence of God. The warrior of the Lord, meek and mild, now as lowly as a lamb replies, 'Father, I dwell in a vile nation, a nation made by your own hand. Many, many in number, even many who say they believe in you Father. But by our deeds and words we deny you constantly, even cursing your Holy name. Truly these things ought not to be. Father we live without the Knowledge of your closeness, and your precious presence. Father this also ought not to be!' Son, please come with me and let us walk in a path never travelled, a place where men never venture! It is the palace of the Fathers house. His royal palace! In His presence we will know as we are truly known! In His presence we will clearly see all things as they are!

The huge door opens, and the warrior steps inside. His inner Heart pauses as He shudders deep within, surveying His surroundings. Yet his stride is not broken. He moves forward with the sureness of a mighty man of valor. He's been in battle before, He knows both sides of the battle well. Soldier to soldier, one on one, face to face. As metal sharpens metal so one man sharpens the other, and both are sharpened! But this day He goes alone.—The vision, the call, the power of the Holy Spirit, Jesus drawing each alone, aside, into the wilderness, the desert, the dark alone! The doors have opened, the man of God inside, seeking command, yes, and counsel for the bride! Marching straight to centre, with a sudden stop to stare, all creation now before him opens! He feels a sudden weakness, as though standing at the precipice! For the sheer vastness before Him He knows that He must bow before the glory of the risen Lord! A word reaches to His heart as he hears creation groaning, and labouring, for the revelation of the sons of God! In this vast place He begins to hear and know His commission to the Lord of Majesty, carrying within His heart the word of reconciliation to God—the word of life—knowing that His master has subjected the creation to futility, in hope! So that she, being in labour groans, until the revelation of the sons of God.

The Lord's Warrior-Reprise

So He stands at the edge of the precipice, gleaming sword in hand. All creation bowing before him awaits the high command. Eternal angels stand in awe, not a breath to take, the shout of glory now to come, The precious bride awakes.

Awake! Awake! Arise O bride hear the glory of your call! Anoint your head with precious oil, Holy Spirit one and all. For thus O bride you must come and stand before my throne, endowed, endued with Holiness, and Holiness alone. In Spirit and in truth you come forsaking one and all! You and you alone must hear the Holy Spirits call.

For you and you alone must rise, and come forsaking all yes, flesh and blood and family forsaking lest you fall. And Satan cannot hinder you if you turn, 'him from,' and leave this evil world behind. For the Father through the Son.

The warrior stands there sword in hand, looks into eternity the lamb upon His throne. Inside his body, trembling with creations final groan.

For it is time for the lambs precious bride to finally come Home.

Its been an epic battle, millions paid the awful toll. The jury seated

Now in heaven, a cloud of witnesses the whole, have seen the battle rage for ages, many soldiers come and gone, but till the final warrior takes His stand the battle rages on.

Not one jot or tittle of the word, be left undone. Every child of God a victor in the battle Christ has won. Many wounded warrior a bloody battle fought, resisting all the evils that Satan's heart has wrought.

To thwart, to twist, to tangle, to snare or even kill. Gods Holy seed the bride of Christ t'was ever Satan's will. But now the final days upon us the time has drawn at last, the final warrior has come in the age of grace to pass. All Satan's fury to be let loose on people down bellow,

All that have rejected God's pure Grace and Holy gospel call. Now the Lord shall descend with the voice of angel's cry, and the trump of God,

The day of grace is over He's coming for His bride.

The Lord's Warrior III

The battle lines have been drawn, so soldier take your sword in
Hand! The sword of the Mighty word of God which is The High command! Hold forth
your shield of faith, as Satan's darts you face, with Holy feet shod with the shoes of
the Gospel of Gods grace. Speaking words of truth your loins girded so, through The
heart of righteousness, where the breastplate must go. Go on O Holy warrior with
Salvation on your head, you are a mighty warrior the enemy's very dread!

I am a warrior! I am a warrior, For Christ's sake, an ambassador for His kingdom.
Sent to reconcile the world to the Father, through the son. The Son of His love, as
Jesus came to reconcile the world to the Father through His own blood. So I seek
to reconcile others to Him through His word.—Thank you Father I go! The warrior
steps into the seething darkness of an evil world, as He goes along his way his path
leads to an old man. A degenerate man, so vile, the warrior in His purity in Christ,
smells and feels deeply the wretched and evil soul that stands before Him.

Sword in hand He holds it forth unto the very heart of as it were the Devil himself,
and presses the Sword of the Spirit deep into His chest. As the fire of the sword
burns the vile, the precious comes, the life comes, where death was life has come.
The old wretched man is transformed in mind, soul, and Spirit. Now crying out
with a purity and Holiness that makes all of Heaven shout ecstatically! I'm alive!
I'm alive! Praise God I'm alive, I was dead, and I didn't Know it. But now I'm
alive. Thank you Jesus! Thank you Jesus!

As I pierced him even His heart I could not have ever known, The glory of my masters
choosing this wicked thing for His own. I stood in awe and trembling as His Spirit
fell, transforming an awful wicked wretch headed straight for hell. His change was
so sudden, and entirely complete, I pierced a vile and wicked man, transformed into
a sheep. He fell down to my feet right then, I too fell there with him, no longer was
he a wretched man, for Jesus now lived in him.

Changed, and changed forever, this is what I saw. I, so awed and bewildered,
gazed at him, then paused. His beauty now so fresh and new, and he so innocent
and pure, after eighty years of wickedness, and this is to be sure. I marvelled, and
almost envied, him so fresh and free, and me a seasoned warrior, bewildered Lord
at thee.

*So many years have come and gone, so many battles lost and won, so many wounds
so deep within, O death where is your victory, O Grave where is your Sting?*

*I saw this portion of the warrior while driving home from work.
It was so intense that I cried over and over while seeing it. I still see it and get all
ripped over it. [ripped] my word for intensely emotional, with tears and crying.*
                    Bless God! Bless God!

The War Counsel

The war counsel was settled at last, the battle plans had all been drawn, the sacrificial lamb had been slain, everything was done. The Generals had all spoken, each one at his turn, not a shadow had been overlooked, not a stone was left unturned.

All was ready and in order, the excitement you could taste, the air around the throne electric, with the burning of His grace. This is why you're here My son, that you too may know, My Holy plan is settled, being set forth long ago. The taste upon your tongue is fire with a metal tinge, how else would you perceive the burning sword within? You are here to learn just what is coming next—the all consuming fire of my righteousness. My bride has been asleep, and taken many lovers to her breast, how does she in soiled garments feign before me righteousness? Here I give her warning, harden not your heart; for the time of battle cries is upon us, to set forth to the mark. To seek my face forever, in all that you must do, to cast away unholy lovers, that you've drawn near to you. To rend your hearts, and not your garments, to humble soul and spirit! I am the Lord, and I change not. And no man can add to it!

The gifting and calling of God are without repentance. God's sword backs up the godly man, preacher, husband, and father as He leads in Spirit and in truth. Today we limit God to the limit of our own minds, as to how we see Him. When in fact, if we only saw a glimpse of Him as He really is, our puny minds would be BLOWN and we would cringe, and collapse to the ground! And the church doesn't even know Him, and that is why we have so many 'professional' christian guru's professing Christ who are twits, and don't know God at all! The first real sign of knowing God is terror. All of the prophets collapsed in the sheer fear of the Lord. I wonder what would happen to most 'peddlers of Christ' if He ever appeared before them while they peddled their quaint, cliche-ick 'witness for Christ' while not knowing Him at all? Any Paul's around? Did you get knocked off of your a—when you met Jesus? Our self-made Apostles and prophets run around and tag the name of JESUS to almost everything that comes into their heads. And if we watch their performance it shouldn't surprise us when we see such a weird Christianity out there.

First step for me—Jesus I want to meet you like Paul did!

Knock me off of my ass-umptions. I don't want to meet you like some peddler or babbler, or some guru, but in reverent fear of the Lord!

Who are you Mr. Wonderful—such and such—person? Don't you know that your grand sum, the total mass and amount of your whole life is Nothing but a mere breath to God? So that you don't measure up to more than a bag of wind? [A little humour here would be nice]—There now doesn't that free you up from a whole lot of pride? Now that you know that you amount to nothing, you can stop the charade and become humble, like a little child and maybe Jesus Christ will save your soul. You who shake your fist at God as if you had something to say to Him! You want to go to Heaven but you don't want God to be there when you get there. Don't you know that God made the heavens and the earth? He breathed them into being! All you breathe out is bad breath and foolish human noise.

To those who shake their fist at God, if they ever got a glimpse of Him, they would probably die or burn right there. That's a close description of the God that made everything that is, and is the owner of it all. You and I included. And you being His property, He could rightly destroy in any way, and still be just and Holy! And even if you thought any different, what could you do to Him . . . ?
Scripture says 'there is no counsel against the Lord!
It's a good day to hear ,fear, and then repent!
The more time we spend taking our masks off before God,
the less time we will spend putting them on before Men.

The wind blew strong and caused the dust to swirl about in small whirlwinds. It was one of these 'hot' August days. Harvest days, when you would breathe and the air was lacking, you would breathe again, still not getting the freshness of the air the body craved.

I walked alone down the dusty deserted road, heart hungry for the freshness of the breath of life.

In this desert of the dog days of August air, I anticipated a sudden, intense change; as though I was about to walk into the Kingdom of God on the Earth. I could taste His approach with the taste of my heart within me. Oh taste and see that the Lord is good! Even now, I still can taste and see that He is good, and the fragrance of His coming is magnificent.

O how does one describe when your whole person goes into the intense groaning, interceding, of the desire, of the flavour, and the fragrance of Christ?

With all my being I speak mysteries to you God, in tongues, with my whole body speaking, yet my mind cannot comprehend.—Still—I desire—Still I seek—Still I watch and pray.—Still, the night is long. . .

Lord come . . . . I wish I could go Lord, you know! I want to go, in the fervent heat of the desire of my inner heart.

Oh hope in God for I shall yet praise Him. My joy and my crown. My friend and my brother. Humble like a child, I stand on the roadside, yeah, it's good.
It's hot, so hot, and dry I see a long road. Your Spirit Lord is
hot within me, drawing me to go forward, compelling me to
enter, to come, to go, to walk, to run, too much Lord!
Too much, yet more! Take me! It's Elijah's whirlwind.
It's Elijah's double portion mantle!
Yes, yes Jesus yes! Where is the God of Elijah! Strike the water! Strike the water!
Stir up the gifts within you. Strike the water. Mighty are you Lord!
God!

The year of unimport

It was the year of unimport in a land not far away,
a very notable fellow they laid to rest that day. The preacher then was speaking,
this he had to say, "Dearly beloved we are gathered here today to send away,
this one time mighty man to his final resting place."
I knew that man of which he spoke, a scoundrel and a cheat, and well could see
him at the throne before the Master's feet.
I heard weeping, gnashing, groaning, and I sensed the pain, the terror of his
judgment, while I heard the preacher say,
"He was a fine man, a good man, and many other lie. As the people all were taken
in—
Oh what a lullaby!
I heard the sound of many waters rushing overhead, and my heart pounded in my
chest from knowing such a dread! This man had gone to face alone the Mighty
Lord of Hosts,
never having ever stopped to put the master first. The terror of his first and final
meeting with our God, screams of horror I could almost hear coming from afar.

O preacher don't you pacify and send them all to hell. Tell the truth of Christ our
Lord, that without Him all will fall, into everlasting torment, torture, and
despair.
Preacher their blood is on your head if you don't even dare, to tell the truth, and
not to lie,
and no one to impress, that every sinner goes to fire, and none of them to rest!

In a vision I saw the man, his judgment now complete, in terror, pain, and
anguish, screaming, with eternal burning, within and without,
in a thousand degrees of
eternal fire and total darkness . . . Many years later, I look again, still I see him
there
not consumed but burning still, not going anywhere! O sinner don't you mock at
Jesus Christ
who you'll meet, for eternal burnings are the future of all the arrogant,
the proud, the rebel, and every liar. Away with all the evil ones, for they are not
of the Father, they are the devil's sons.

So bow your heads, and do repent, confess to Jesus Christ your sins, and your judgment He'll relent! But if you continue in your sinful way, know this for certain then,
in fire you will pay for every, every sin . . . .

The Witness

In the process of time and in the course of events, oh goodly Gentlemen, God has seen fit to take unto Himself the bride, whom He has longed for these many centuries. It was His doing, and marvelous in His eyes, not that these whom He has taken had been 'ever perfect'. But at once when they finally perceived Him to whom they were betrothed, the precious Christ, who bore them at the place of death, they steadfast and quickly arose, and made themselves ready—washing in the blood of the Lamb—"Christ". Then adorned themselves in the purest of wedding gown. The sparkling white robe of the righteousness of Jesus. Thus She had purified Herself. So at the time of readiness, she truly was a pure and spotless bride, completely without spot or wrinkle.

Long before their removal however, they were often time the most out of place of all people that you could imagine. They talked about this Jesus, in whom they said they believed, and even I believed in this Jesus that they spoke of. He I Instinctively knew was true. But they evidenced such a coldness toward outsiders that I could not get over it! Oh they often spoke of the Lord, but He seemed harsh at times, and judgmental. I suppose a God who is Holy would have to judge somewhat harshly. But again by instinct, I knew that this God, even their 'God', must be a merciful and forgiving God. Hadn't He forgiven so many of them? And some of the things that they had done even when they were "saved" [as they said.] Anyway, I could not get past the things they did and there seemed to be such a pride about them. And some put on an air of humility that seemed so rotten; I don't know! It just didn't add up you know? And it always seemed like this Jesus they talked about was so far away. Many times being around them they would say things they believed, because their Bible said it. But watching and listening to them you knew that they really weren't sure about 'many' things at all. I guess that that is why they acted and talked the way they did. I suppose the worlds impact on their eyes and ears—you know, the violent movies, all kinds of perversions, 'startling' scientific discoveries, and technologies. I suppose they too were a bit fooled as we were into thinking this is it! You know, the great frontier of the mind of Man! A conqueror of "all". But Man! We could never conquer death! No matter what men did to try to stop it, death came to all, making every accomplishment and every endeavor seem so pointless! You know that is' 'one' thing that I remember some of them said, 'the bolder ones' always said, "The wages of sin is death! And that all men die and then comes the judgment." So somehow I understood that all of death comes from sin, and all men sin, so death comes to all men. Listen to me! No technology or science could ever change the fact of Death!

Except: ~ This one man who they spoke of 'Jesus'- Who came to earth as a man, born of a woman, but without an earthly Father; Did not inherit sin and death, but they said He became death for us, that is He became sin for us, in that He bore our sins on the cross! And since death had no power over Him, He being sinless, conquered sin and death and arose from the dead. My friends, this is one thing that they all knew! They always spoke of this as a surety, not ever doubting it at all! Even their children knew this, as well as the most timid of their number.

They spoke of Jesus coming back in the clouds, as He left; and His taking to Himself His bride which is the Church. Now you know as well as I do, that for most of the time since Christianity began, these people at times seemed way more confused than the remainder of us who knew no God at all. Thus they did not live up to the standard that their claims seemed to require. It was all quite puzzling, until a short while before they all disappeared. It seemed to me that all of those I knew who followed the 'way' of Christ finally saw, or knew, who they were and where they were going. Then everything changed! They became 'so Real' in their faith and so full of love and kindness. Some hated them the more, but some who had hated them before were, swept right into their number. I remember that there was an awesome sense of glory, love, and grace that followed them whereever they went. I became convinced that whoever this God, this Jesus was, that He is Real. And I know even today that He is Real. Because I have known many people in my life, and I noticed that men don't change. They just don't! And here all of these people, suddenly changed, and for the better! This also is unheard of, and very contrary to nature, and to men. With this change there came an awesome sense of the fear of God! Almost as if He were suddenly going to rip open the sky and present Himself to a world of people who thought that the universe was so vast that nothing could ever harm or alter it. But I was there, when the fearsome sense of God's presence was such as if He would tear open the sky right above us and that we would see His face. It seemed that many would die from the fear of what would happen. Their hearts stopping in their chest, from the fear of this God.

Now as for me, I don't say that I believe, as Christians used to say, but I say this-I know! That the God who made everything is much Greater than all of the things that He made! ~ I know that I am fearful of Him. Who, even though I didn't know Him, made Me and gave Me life. ~ I know that I am subject to His will, I confess that I willingly submit to His Authority. ~ I know my master, He is God! And I know, His Son Jesus, 'The Christ'. So if you choose to end My life for my confession of faith in Christ Jesus, I have but this to say . . . Father, forgive them, they know not what they do! And Father, for the joy set before Me, I endure even thi . . . .

It is said that today we live in a post Christian era but we have news for those who would say this! Because every era belongs to God! Without question, whether men believe or not . . . Every man may shake his fist at God, but in His time He will come, and all those who oppose Him will look to the rocks to fall on them, to hide them from His face! . . . I think Christians are so caught up in the day-to-day run of life that they forget to remember- the coming of the Lord is at hand! Our God who is the creator of the universe does not need permission from men, 'whom He created', to invade it and to put an end to any of its inhabitants.

[Yes God did put the earth under the Authority of Men.] But only until He returns! Then He will put an end to the ways of men, and will Rule His Kingdom in Righteousness.

. . . As The bible says in one place: "Let God be true and every man a liar! Father, in this world I pray, Lord let your Holy will be done, even among the people of my nation. Lord do it. Amen.

Then the Lord answered

Then the LORD answered _Your name_ out of the whirlwind, and said; Who is this who darkens counsel by words without knowledge? Now prepare yourself like a Man; I will question you, and you shall answer Me. Where were you when I laid the foundations of the Earth? Tell Me if you have understanding. Who determined it's measurements? Surely you know! Or who stretched the line upon it? To what were it's foundations fastened? Or who laid it's cornerstone, when the morning stars sang together, and all the Sons of God shouted for Joy? Or who shut in the sea with doors, when it burst forth and issued from the womb; When I made the clouds it's garment, and thick darkness it's swaddling band; When I fixed my limit for it, and set bars and doors; when I said, 'this far you may come, but no farther, and here your proud waves must stop!' Have you commanded the morning since your days began, and caused the dawn to know it's place, That it might take hold of the ends of the earth, and the wicked be shaken out of it? It takes on form like clay under a seal, and stands out like a garment. From the wicked their light is withheld, and the upraised arm is broken. Have you entered the springs of the sea? Or have you walked in search of the depths? Have the gates of Death been revealed to you? Or have you seen the doors of the shadow of death? Have you comprehended the breadth of the Earth? Tell Me, if you know all this. Where is the way to the dwelling of light? And darkness, where is it's place, that you may take it to it's territory, that you may know the paths to its home? Do you know it because you were born then, or because the number of your days is great? Have you entered the treasury of the snow, or have you seen the treasury of hail, which I have reserved for the time of trouble, for the day of battle and war? By what way is light diffused, or the east wind scattered over the earth? Who has divided a channel for the overflowing water, or a path for the thunderbolt, to cause it to rain on a land where there is no one, a wilderness where there is no man; To satisfy the desolate waste, and to cause to spring forth the growth of tender grass? Has the rain a Father? Or who has begotten the drops of dew? From whose womb comes the ice? And the frost of Heaven who gives it birth? The waters harden like a stone, and the surface of the deep is frozen. Can you bind the cluster of Pleiades, or lose the belt of Orion? Can you bring out Mazzaroth in its season? Or can you guide the great bear with its cubs? Do you know the ordinances of the heavens? Can you set their dominion over the earth? Can you lift up your voice to the clouds, that an abundance of waters may cover you? Can you send out lightning's, that they may go, and say to you, 'here we are!'? Who has put wisdom in the mind? Or who has given understanding to the heart? Who can number the clouds by wisdom? Or who can pour out the bottles of heaven, when the dust hardens in the clumps, and the clods cling together? Can you hunt the prey for the lion, or satisfy the appetite of the young lions, when they crouch in their dens, or lurk in their lairs to lie in wait? Who provides food for raven, when it's young ones cry to God, and wonder about for lack of food?—

Moreover the Lord answered _your name_, and said: "Shall He who contends with the Almighty correct Him? He who rebukes God let him answer it." Then _____ answered the Lord and said: Behold, I am vile; What shall I answer you? I lay my hand over my mouth. Once I have spoken, but I will not answer; yes, twice, but I will proceed no further. Then _____ answered the Lord and said: I know that you can do everything, and that no purpose of yours can be withheld from you. You asked, 'who hides counsel without knowledge'? Therefore I have uttered what I did not understand, Things too wonderful for me, which I did not know. Listen please and let me speak; You said 'I will question you, and you shall answer me.'
"I have heard of you by the hearing of the ear, But now my eye see's You. Therefore I abhor myself, and repent in dust and ashes."

This is the account of Job in Job 38 and part of 39 and 40. The blanks are for you and I to personalize the message which God gave to Job, by placing our name's there.

In the arrogance and pride of our humanity we revel in ignorance of God. Taken to heart, Job is greatly humbled by God and so will we be 'if' we allow ourselves the luxury of thought and meditation, in other words 'give our head a shake' and repent, waking up as Ephesians says 'for Christ to shine on us.'

THERE IS NO HILL THAT
I NEED TO CLIMB

There is no hill that I need to climb, no valley to walk through
No rocky waters that I'd like to cross, Lord I just want to be with you
In Spirit and in truth you are, where I want to be
Nothing in this world to want, or do I need to see
My eyes behold you Lord, you are everything to me
That's all there is and nothing more, you are where I want to be
This is not a lamentation, no Lord I would rejoice
For truly I desire to see your Holy face, and to hear your voice
No mountains left before me now, only one great plain to cross
this world of flesh and blood, to glory in you Lord

THY KINGDOM COME!

Not my will but thine be done,
Not my kingdom, but thy kingdom come.
My will I will your way. Father take my will
Today. In Jesus Holy name I pray, amen.

There are two fires in the word of God
Both are eternal
Neither will ever be quenched
One is the Glory of God
[the all consuming fire]
which refines, and purifies and is
also at the judgment seat of Christ!

The other is the fire of Hell, the lake of fire.
Where they are never consumed, and their worm never dies.

Everyone ever born into this human world will dwell within
one or the other forever. So if your brand of Christianity, or religion, or
even rebellion toward God—exclude Gods purging Holy fire, or any
aspect of His word—Find Him! I guarantee it will Hurt! But when
His fire burns brightly in your heart you will know like every real believer
'It's all that is worth anything in all of creation.'

Nothing comes close to the Glory of "knowing" Christ Jesus in your Heart!
Nothing!

You will never need to fire proof your life—If—His holy fire—is—your life
And If it is not—you Can't stop Him—You belong to this God who is God.
Like it or Not!

So if you are His enemy, remember His fire is coming to you—Soon—maybe
before you know it!
Repent! Repent and believe the Gospel.

Those who are asleep in Christ shall [wake up] at the resurrection as Adam did at His creation. Complete and whole. No flaw or fault, no sin or shame. For the first man 'Adam' became a living soul, the last Adam 'Jesus' became a life giving Spirit. As Jesus said "the Spirit is life, the flesh profits Nothing" Those who are born of the Spirit, shall never see, or taste death. Those in the flesh are dead 'already', though they live. As Paul the Apostle said, to live is Christ, to die is gain. This is my desire this is my hope, to be dead to sin, and to the world, and to be alive to God, through the cross of Jesus Christ. Therefore if any man is in Christ he is a new creation, created in Christ Jesus, never to taste death, hell, or the grave. Oh grave where is your victory, oh death where is your sting? Victory over death, has for all been accomplished, if Men would but see their nakedness Your carnal flesh means nothing to God, as well as your self made righteousness, He is God, He knows what it takes to make a man alive, and live. I'm telling you today my friend today, no man can make it without Him, We all 'must' be born again.

To Radical?

*Show me your faith without works, and I'll show you my faith by my
works, for as the body without the Spirit is dead so also faith without
works is dead, being by itself.*

*I'm a Christian many say but did you feed a man today? I'm a Christian,
you might guess, Did you, your enemy today bless? I'm a Christian, don't you
know? Can you tell it by my clothes? I'm a Christian, you can see, showing of
                                       your
nice RV, and your boat, and your jeep, and all of you mountains of felt needs.
I'm a Christian you can tell, cause I never say the word for—ell.
I'm a Christian this I know for my preacher tells me so. He even calls over to
my house if ever a Sunday I should miss.*

*Why do you ask my friend?
Well I've been observing you, and I wonder what to do?
I don't have a house or boat, no motor home, or any tote.
When I travel it's by foot, I don't have far to go.*

*I truly, truly hope I'm saved and go to Jesus 'on that day' That's the only hope
I have, and nothing in this world. But to love my lord.*

Un masked

The more time we spend taking our masks off before God,

the less time we will spend putting them on before Men.

Unforgiveness puts us into the same prison as the one's we are keeping there, because we have to guard the cell door to make sure they don't get out . . . all the while they probably are not aware that they are in our prison, leaving us—alone there in our own Jail.

Until somebody comes Home.

You can heal the sick, raise the dead, and give sight to the blind! But, it isn't real until sombody comes back home, coming home to God. [To Jesus Christ] in spirit and in truth. That is real! That is healing, that is salvation, and life! There is no future without Christ. Christ 'in you' is the hope of glory. Oh won't you understand this?

Oh Father, my Father you are so true, your words are true, all your ways are true, but we have walked in such a shallow understanding of you that we have barley gotten our feet wet, in the river of the living water of God. And we have been living in annoyance, being annoyed with damp socks, when we have wanted to swim in the river of your delight. We haven't known you Father. We thought we were altogether like you, but we have been blind, and leaders of the blind, and the ditches around us are full. Father please have mercy on us your children. Pull us out of this brackish water, and wash us and fill us to overflowing, with the pure water the wellsprings of the living water of life. Open our eyes that we might see, and give us ears that hear. Heal us Oh lord, and we will be healed. Save us and we will be saved. amen.

Wait on the lord, call upon him with all of your heart.
Trust him and seek his face. For to those who seek him with
'All' their heart, he will be found.
He will not be found in the form's and traditions of man made religion's,
No! He won't be found in houses of pretenders, or in denomination's of carnal,
Sensuous men who are god in their own minds, or who's god is made up of their own imaginations.
Or those who's faith is in their 'opinion' no.
He will however be found by anyone who can crash through all of these mountains of
'Philo—psyco—human systematic, and sympathetic delusions—to humble their own flesh, and
Cry out to God for truth. He is the only one. There is no other.
Blessed are those who seek him.
Jesus is the way, the truth, and the life.
There is no other way, or truth, or life. If you have christ alive in you
You have life, if you don't have him 'alive' in you, you don't have life.
This is truth that Christ came to save sinners of which I am chief
In him is everlasting life. No longer seek men, or doctrine's of men, or teachings, or teachers,

But look unto the Lord of glory and receive forgiveness for every sin, and the outcome everlasting life

Wait

We are a generation of entertainment, and self pleasure gluttons!
I want it, and I want it 'now' if it feels good, tastes good, or looks good,
If I like it, its ok! Where is christian dedication, moral attitude, tenacity, and fervour?
Where indeed is the Church? Church is not a place to go church is a people to be!

Welcome To My World

Welcome to my world, welcome to my happy song;
Where it's all about me, But I'm so glad you came along;
Welcome to my life, don't talk to me of sacrifice, of giving of myself, and life for
the sake of Jesus Christ.
I know that He loves me—just look at all I have, I know that I am blessed, more
than any other man.
A mansion on the hill, I don't need at all, I own so much of this world, I have no
need at all.
So welcome to my world, jump right into my show.
I have a bright red wagon, the best in town I know.
It's always about me, all about the myself show.
Don't tell me about self-sacrifice, or of rocky narrow roads.
I've heard it all before, I'm not listening anymore.
I found "this Jesus is my Lord." I've got so much that I can't want more!

I know you say you're rich, cause Jesus Lives in you, But I see you live like this,
a wooden shack and worn out shoes, I see you have no car, no cell phone or computer
too, to see the whole wide world, O I have more than you!
Now why're you cryin there, on your knees and prayin;
That God would take away these things, I don't know what to say!
If I get the time some day, I suppose that I may bow my knees to pray for you,
that He would make you wise—to earn such as I.

Yet you say, "No way. I'm already rich.
Today this stove box is my perfect home,
I'd be glad to be alone, Just leave me here to pray,
In two minutes I'll be on His throne,
In Spirit and in truth, more glorious than you!
For I have found the way to the greatest riches every day,
that's being before His throne and glorying in Christ alone,
He really is the only way."

What A Wonder!

Yeshua [Jesus] said once 'I thank you Father that you have hidden these things from the "wise" and have shown them to the naive'

Here my friends is what He showed me last night:

Holy, means separate, pure, clean, and set—apart.

separate, different, completely different! Not at all like the rest. 'Set apart.'

What?—You say

You say there's nothing going on, nothing fresh and new,
nothing really happening between the Lord and you.
So you go and throw your brain into a world of selfish pleasures,
into a vat of vain pursuits of your own endeavours.
Then you thing to come back to Him as His pure and spotless bride.—Not one
moment have you stopped to look so deep inside.

Well I don't know about that, think I've got news for you . . . Jesus knows just
what's inside, and all you say and do. And he's callin us each and every one to
abandon this world of flesh and come, to walk in eternity with the Father's Son.

So go and get your heart back from wherever you have sent it, and give it back to
Jesus. Find your treasure in His stead, and let the saviour fill it, then, 'you will
always have something going on something fresh and new.'

Jesus will be in your heart in all you say and do, and when you come to stand
before His holy throne, you will be there happy that you lived for Christ alone.
This is the only thing on earth you really need to know, take Jesus with every
everywhere you Go . . . and your treasure will be in Him, and forever in his
kingdom. amen . . .

What is Idolatry? Can Christians get it? Is it fatal if they do?
Everything that you do without Christ as your hearts focus.
Idolatry is leaving His kingdom to live in your own.
No not even the worlds, but your own!

Jesus said, I am the way. The truth and the life. And
You must love the Lord with all your heart, and soul,
And mind, and strength. If He's got something going on inside of
You, you'll always have a 'testimony' too.

What can happen in One day?

What can happen in one Day? Everything you know can pass away! The mountains can all crumble, And fall flat to the ground. The valleys can be heaved up, high as level ground, What can happen in one day? Many things it seems, Nation's, kingdoms, countries, Forever perishing . . . What can happen in one day? The Son be darkened, as the night, all the elements could melt. What could happen in one day? Maybe men could catch a thought of what is coming next.

Say that you are young, married fresh and new, suddenly the whole world shifts, and starts and everything's shook loose. All the houses are destroyed, not one of them is left. No more Walmart, Superstore, or McDonalds left. All the Government is extinct, Hospitals all gone, no more motor vehicles, trucks or busses to ride on. Many others I could say, I think you get the point . . . everything you knew and loved is forever gone.

As survivors now you two are left to the work at hand, to work with sweat upon your brow to get a living from the land. So one day you bring forth a child and you watch him grow, then you sit when he is older and tell of long ago. Son you may not believe this but we used to own a house, a truck, and a car, we used to drive along the highway at sixty miles per hour. We used to walk across the street, and buy our groceries from the store. Then we'd bring them home and put them in the refrigerator. We used to go to the airport every now and then, and climb into a Jet and fly of to another land. Son this world is all you've ever known but once upon a time, 'One day' happened , everything changed and we were left behind. A lot can happen in one day, now we've come to know it. Hold your life with a loose grip for God may make you let it go.

But He says to you what ever is a car? And what is this other thing for food, a refrigerator? Well son a refrigerator is like a great big box, Whoa! what's a box? Maybe you've been laying for too long with your head on that damp moss!

*No son, a box was made of cardboard, and cardboard from a tree. I told
you at the start son that you might not believe me. A lot can happen
in one day, the world as we now know it could forever change,
and change again, like it did in the time of Noah.*

*For as it was in the days of Noah so it shall be
in the days of the Son of man.*

What Can I Write

What can I write Lord in your sight?
What word to place before your face?
And who am I before your eyes that I ought to
stand and face you Oh God? You see right through me, nothing
at all to hide. You know my way. Every molecule, every DNA.
No science will hide, or close your eyes! No screaming noises
of angry cries, will ever close you outside of any heart.
You are the 'start' the chisel that chips away
the stony heart and stiff neck that I have made,
cutting through apostasy bringing a burning flame!
How can I stand before your gaze, and try to look upon your face?
I wish to run and try to hide, no place to go you've broke inside.
You are right there Crash course comes with you, head on collision what
can I do? So deep inside I feel the tear, as a lion on His prey.
Where can I run to get away, from the fire burning in me?
I am alive this I know is true, I feel the fire, Lord it's you!

What If An Ungodly Man Went To Heaven?

What if an ungodly man went to Heaven?
Every man who has his hope in Christ purifies Himself. 1 John 3:3
This article was written 300 or so years ago by a puritan pastor named J.C. Ryle.
Suppose and ungodly man went to Heaven:

Suppose for a moment that you were allowed to enter Heaven without Holiness. What would you do there? What possible enjoyment could you possibly feel there? To which of all the saints would you join yourself to, and by who's side would you sit?

Their pleasures are not your pleasures. Their tastes are not your tastes. Their Character, not your character. How could you possibly be happy in heaven if you had not been Holy on Earth?

-Now you love the company of the frivolous and the careless. The worldly minded, and the covetous, the reveler and the pleasure seeker, the ungodly, and the profane. There will be none such in Heaven. Now you think that the people of God are strict, and particular, and serious, you rather avoid them, you have no delight in their society. But remember there will be no other company in Heaven. Now you think that praying, and scripture reading, and Hymn singing are dull and melancholy, and stupid work. Remember that the inhabitants of Heaven rest not day and night saying Holy, Holy, Holy Lord God almighty, and singing the praises of the Lamb. How could an unholy man find pleasure in such an environment as this? An unholy man would feel like a stranger in a land he knew not. A black sheep amidst Christ's pure flock. The song of angels, and of Ark angels, and the congregation of Heaven would be a language he cold not understand. The very air would seem, air he could not breathe. I know not what others think, but to me it does seem clear that Heaven would be a miserable place to an unholy man. It cannot be otherwise.

People may say in a vague way, that they hope to go to Heaven when they die, but surely they do not consider what they say! We 'Must' be Heavenly minded, and have Heavenly tastes in the present life, or else we shall never find ourselves in Heaven in the life to come. Are you Holy? I don't ask whether you attend your church regularly. Whether you were baptized, whether you profess to be a Christian. Are You yourself Holy this very day, or are you Not?

Why do I ask so straight, and pose the question so strongly? I do it because the scripture says that without Holiness No man will see the Lord. It is written, it is not my private opinion. The word of God, not of Man. Without Holiness No man shall see the Lord. Hebrews 12:14

Alas what searching sifting words are these. I look at the world and I see the greater part of it lying in wickedness. I look at professing Christians and see the vast majority having nothing of Christianity, but the mere name. I turn to the bible and I hear the Spirit saying WITHOUT Holiness No man shall see the Lord. Surely it is a text which ought to make solemnly consider our 'way's', and search our Heart. You may say if you were so Holy would be unlike other people. I answer 'I know it well'. It is just what you ought to be. Christ's true servants were always unlike the world around them. A holy nation, a separate people. And you must be so too, If you would be saved. You may say, at this rate very few will be saved. I answer I know it well. It is precisely what Jesus told us in His sermon on the mount. Straight is the Gate, and narrow is the way which leads to life, and few there are who find it. Few will be saved because few will take the trouble to seek Salvation. Men will not deny themselves the pleasures of sin for a little season. You may say these are hard sayings, the way is very narrow. I know it is, the Lord Jesus said so eighteen hundred years ago. He always said that men must take up the cross daily, and that they must be ready to cut off hand or foot if they would be his Disciples. That Religion which costs Nothing, is worth NOTHING. J.C. Ryle 17TH Century puritan pastor.

My note: If your faith doesn't cost you Everything, It's worth Nothing!
If you think that you ready to meet God, you are far from ready.
If you think that you can want anything, or anyone other than the Kingdom of God and still be His, Think –again— but this time, be sure to Think.
Lord save us I pray. Wake us up. Amen.

What Jesus said . . .

Repent and believe. Repent and be converted. Repent and be baptized. He who believes will be saved. Those who believe and are baptized will be saved.

Come out from among them, be separate, and I shall be your God and you shall be my people. This people Honour me with their lips but their Heart is far from Me. Go into all the world and preach, and make disciples. These signs will follow those who believe. They will cast out Demons they will speak with new tongues. they will take up serpents and they will not harm them.

Jesus laid it all down straight. If you abide in My word, and My word abides in you, My Father and I will abide in you. He who comes to God must believe that He is and that He is the rewarder of those who diligently seek Him. I am your exceeding great reward {He says}

Because abiding in Christ, and Christ abiding in you is the 'only' reward that is eternal, and the only reward that is worth anything.

My crown of glory, and my pearl of greatest price is Christ 'in Me' 'the hope of glory'. Christ in Me, He is my all in all. Christ in Me 'He is the life' Christ in me from glory to glory, to the fullness of the stature of the measure of Christ. And if I have eyes that see, and ears that hear, and the body rejects the eyes, then the eyes are alone and are helpless, and the body is left blind. Christ in you is the only hope of glory. Paul said 'if for this life only we have faith, we are of all people the most pity-able! This people sit down to eat, and rise up to play. My house shall be a house of prayer. 'I am the exceeding great reward'- if you abide in My words. If anyone loves Me he will keep my words, and we will come to Him and make our home with Him. But the helper, the Holy Spirit, whom the Father will send in my name, He will teach you all things, and bring to your remembrance all things that I said to you.

Lord Give us ears that really hear I pray amen.

What kind of faith

What kind of faith do I have, that cannot change my way?

That cannot heal my body, that cannot heal my soul?

What kind of faith do we have that cannot preach the truth?

That cannot boast in Christ alone, and can do nothing for the youth?

What kind of faith do we have that cannot reach a single one, and cannot feed a famished soul,

that cannot touch the nations, and cannot make a blind man whole?

What kind of faith do we have when we cannot pray,

stay up all night and plead with God that He would heal our Land,

and make straight our way?

Lord Jesus, I pray give me faith. Give me strength,

Let your words be powerful in me, and teach me to pray.

What Should I write the cross in sight,
And who should be upon it?
You or Me upon that tree,
Which one of us has earned it?

I see some stains when I look at you,
But too well I know you see mine too!
So what ever should both I and you
Really seek to see? Except the broken
Body of one dear soul, who paid the
Total awful toll, for you and also for me!

No longer look upon my sins, no longer
Hover there, you're not so lofty and without stain
When laid open, stripped and bare!
And I too should only dare to see whatever sin
Is left in me,
And choose to think within myself,
Lord thank you that I'm healed.

What would happen if we all 'suddenly woke up'?

We would see God as 'He is', rather than as we have been politically, philosophically, and psychologically lead to believe. Not only that, but traditionally, familiarly, romantically, and even seductively—to see Him.

All our pet Me-isms, our jangle and shallow Jesus talk, our pseudo-Christianity, our phoniness would violently implode! For God is an all consuming fire!

We would stagger, stumble, and fall before the true Gospel of Christ. The real stumbling block
of the whole earth by which we 'must' be saved! Totally changed!

We would see Christ as He really is! And ourselves as we really are.
Some would truly repent and turn to the God of Israel in Spirit and in truth. But I feel that
most would flat out reject Him still! Preferring their own paths of self-worship.

This day will come—when they can no longer pretend, and they will cry out for the rocks to fall on them to hide them from the wrath of the Lamb. If these were not the pretenders, how would they know that the wrath is from the Lamb, or who the Lamb is? 'The Lion of Judah is also the Lamb of God.'

If we suddenly woke up, we would see a complete global domination plan in action, right now, and that our freedom is only an illusion.

Commerce is an all consuming snare. Also self-pleasure, and the classic American dream, which will show itself to be a nightmare in the end. There is so much more! We have been controlled and deceived by society, government, selfishness, and greed!

If we don't know or believe that God will supply our every need according to His riches in Christ Jesus,
we are easily drawn to covet both the things that we have and the things that we don't have.
This locks us into Idolatry. Even if you don't agree—self—preservation is also idolatry.

Jesus said hate your life and you will find it if you lose it for His sake.

Open my eyes Lord Jesus!

Jesus said over 2000 years ago 'this is an adulterous and idolatrous generation.'
Two complete and perfect descriptions of our global populace today. Have Mercy
on us! Oh God!

All of the people of the earth are very religious—Unbelief is a state of faith in
self, and of humanism, which denies God, who is Not an opinion, nor open to
opinion, or interpretation.

If one is stuck on interpretation, he is proud and knows nothing. Men don't
interpret scripture, or God!
Scripture reveals God in Spirit and in truth!

Our philosophical brand of Christianity has made us an opinionation-nation and
we think God can't or won't act. He will!

If every Christian were Real, there would be global revival—only because God
would be Honored among His own!

Our so called Honor of Him belittles Him and dishonors Him to the degree that
He fits our lies and philosophies.

If we knew Him we would worship Him in the dirt! Truly! And we would
despise ourselves, even unto death, as Job did.

Man don't we get it?

[No-te-stoe]

Oh God! You are Real!

When!

When all of the works of the day are done, and all the worship songs are sung,
When all of the praying Lord is through, and the Holy Ghost praying too,
When I'm left alone on my bed and the sleep I long for escapes me, When the pain of
Loneliness crushes my heart, and draws mournful tears from my eyes. I stare off into the
Darkness of my room, my heart groaning from the absurdity of so much loss. My Lord,
My God! What, what, what now? What do you want Me to do? Aaaaagh Lord what?
Still I wait still I wonder, Lord am I a fool and not a man? What, what, what, of this man Lord? What of this man, what ever shall become of Him? Whenever will It end?
Will tomorrow find Him well or will these chains still hold him captive to the thing he cannot change?—Wait! God is light in Him there is no darkness at all! What then? Return!
Yes return to the strong hold of life, and rejoice in the stronghold of Joy! In returning and rest you shall be saved, in quietness and confidence shall be your strength! Return to the stronghold of hope. Though the enemy come at me one way, through God He will flee
seven. So I return. Reviled I bless, persecuted I resign to Christ, Cast down I am not destroyed, not returning evil for evil, but overcoming evil with good, that good may overtake all in Christ Amen!

When darkness overwhelms me, no light to be found
I call upon your name Lord as I seek for Holy ground.
I seek a place of sanctuary, where no enemy can come in,
And when I am alone with you, I know that I have found
My hiding place, and I know that you are all in all to me.
I slip my sandals from my feet as I approach you there,
Lord I look into your Holy face and I become aware,
That your all in all to me. I glory in Your presence,
You are all in all to me.

When I bow before you throne humbled by your Majesty

I know that you are here, and your all in all to me.
And I'm glad Lord at your feet, and I surrender all,
I am as one who's died when I behold you Lord.
For I am crucified when I'm beholding you, you are all in all to me and I glory in
your presence, what else could I do,
What else can I say, but your all in all to Me.

I lay down my gilding sword, as I approach you
There, I look upon your face O Lord and am ever more aware, that you are all in
all to me.

I see the glory of the Lord in the land of the living. This is
My hope, and my desire 'in my life' to see men come
To the Lord, Humbling themselves, and repenting
For their deeds against God, who is, and is all in all . . . amen

When fire raged against me lord,
You held me in your hand . . . And when
I was caught up in a stormy blast,
You helped me lord to stand . . . And when all my hopes and dreams gave way
troubles to the of this world, and it seemed to me that I was all alone like a
broken little child, lord you held on tightly to me, no you didn't let me go, you
never did give up on me, my life to you I owe . . . When the fire raged upon my
heart, and I didn't understand, lord I held on to your holy name, and you held
onto my hand, I held onto your holy name and you held onto my hand.

When I called you did not come,
When alone where did you run?
I sought for you through day and
Night, I called to you, you turned
In flight, oh what a wonder son,
That you do not hear though I
Speak into your ear? What is the
Wall between us now? Is it your
Faith that vanishes? I have called,
You did not come, for many years
Now son, my son. But you are mine
I'll not decline to take, and cleanse
You clean. I'll set your feet on Holy
Ground and wash you Deep within.
This world, from which you come
Is putrid, filth and bare, few are they
That listen son and fewer still that
Hear! My kingdom is not of that world
The world of swine's delight, where men
And women of all kinds live only for their
Sight. For what they see, and what they
Want, and for what to wear, this is not
The reason that I placed people there!
Soon 'I am', is coming to reclaim His own
I'll be coming in great clouds to take
My precious home. So tarry in the place
I put you, and there be salt and light,
I will not tarry to return, I may come tonight.
In a moment I'll return, the twinkling of
An eye, and cut my work short in righteousness
The moment Son draws nigh! Hold On!
Be faithful till the end and you will receive
The crown of righteousness, I'm your reward,
Brother, lover, and Best friend. A servant does not know
What his master is doing therefore I have called you
Friend.

Where evil abounds Grace abounds still more.
I ask Lord for your mercy, my soul driven to
The floor. The ground around is mire from all
Of my wailing and my tears, and all my days are
Hidden from me, I know not moments, days,
Or years . . . but still I know I trust you, that you will
Bring me out of evils horrid presence,
with grace shining all about

Where there is a will

Where there is a will there is a
way. Let thy will be mine today.
Let thy will Lord, become mine

Can anyone thus say amen, then
say it once, and once again!

So shout it out so loud and clear and let this
whole wide world so hear!

His Kingdom come His will be
done the only everlasting one, He
is the way, truth, and the life,
His kingdom has arrived.

Where the Spirit Is There Is Life, I Know You'll Rightly Say
'Where the Spirit is there is liberty' ...

Well said... Jesus says the same, in His eternal word.
To true too 'where the Spirit is there is life'. Scripture says
Without the spirit the Body dies. Paul also said In Romans
If the Spirit that raised Christ from the dead dwells in
You, Christian.... That same Spirit who raised Jesus from the dead will give Life
to your mortal body. The body without the Spirit is dead, dead. If the Spirit of
Christ dwells in us
-The Church-, the Christians, that Same Spirit will give life to The Body? Are we
real? I mean 'are we real'? Does Father God look at us and say in His heart 'Ah
my children love me so much?' Or does He see that we don't know Him in truth at
all and that for the most part our Christianity is a mere mantra that we constantly
chirp at one another, in order to comfort, and console ourselves?
What do you expect would happen to 'YOU' if God, suddenly tore open the sky
right about where you were standing right about. Now! Is the Jesus you believe in
going to be able to protect you? Will he be able to save you?

Or is 'your' Jesus a Bar-Jesus? Or a Philosophical Jesus?
Were you born again, were you converted, 'changed' when you believed? Did Jesus
Christ really do something in you?

Were you baptized? Did you receive the Holy Ghost, and tongues when you believed?
Were you born again of the Spirit of God?
Or did you just start going to church?
If any man be in Christ he is a new creature the Old has passed away, buried with
Christ in baptism. raised up with Christ into newness, the eternal, everlasting life
of the Spirit. God says in Isaiah, My ways are higher than yours, and my thoughts
are higher than yours.... I wonder if we are looking High enough... Maybe some
of us should,
Walk on water, and heal the sick and preach the gospel,
Even out of church...

Why I write

It's not in me to make a show, or to be someone that I don't know
my desire is to go home to be with Christ the only, all in all.

When I was small a little child I knew Him then, then I grew wild, following
each worldly whim
I lost my path, and walk with Him.

So this day I'd let you know the things I write are not for show, except that I
might tell to all
That Jesus Christ is all in all.

No other path is there to walk, no other way, no other talk. He is the life the
only one, He
is the Lord the Fathers son.

Its not for me that I write these things, but that somehow someone Might hear
Jesus speak to their own heart as they read
what's written here.

Will you honour Him?

Who will you worship?

Will you worship you?

Oh Father, oh father Give us eyes to see who it is that we truly live for

forgive us this great wrong for we do not know you.

Have mercy on this earth, Lord only the people whom you have made in your own image and likeness are capable of rejecting you.

You Lord in the beginning have made us to be just like you, only just a bit lower than the angels.

Wrong place

Yeah, I'm in the wrong place when, I cannot see Your face,
When all that lies before me is of the Human race.
Cars, and boats, and airplanes. Smoke screens of all kinds.
Friendly folks, and neighbours, family so fine.
Whatever did You come for, Lord, life is just so fine!
Fishing, hunting, family, Why do I feel so blind?
Something deep within me says throw it all away!
I am the truth, I am the life, Son—I am the way!
A long time now I am seeing, that there 'must' be a part,
A big piece of eternity that's been missing from my heart.
To know You is life my Lord, I know You are the way,
Yet, I know that I am missing You still this very day!
Whatever is this blindness that keeps me in the dark?
Whatever should I do? And should I run, how far?
Crushed! Yes, severely broken, aching, staggering in my heart,
I cry to You, I look to You, Lord Jesus.
How far? How far? Broken and battered. O my God, You are!
My heart pants and thirsts for You! Save me! My dear heart.
Truly I waste away, while the wickedest of my enemies say come to me let's play.
For we sit down to eat, and rise up to play, over, and over, and over again!
But in my heart I pray, "Save me Lord from my closest friend, whoever would
draw me away."
For a brother is born for adversity, and fun at times is fine,
but the Road is hard and treacherous, which leaves this wilderness behind!

Ye must be born again

Ye must be born again, my friend O please
Now won't you hear it. The treasure of this flesh life is, that there is nothing to it!
For flesh gives birth to flesh and there is no reward, for anything gained within
This world that's
Separate from the Lord.
What must this babbler be saying, what's he speaking of
For all men know were all OK we have the Fathers love!
For God so loved the world it says, that's all we really
Need
But Jesus said repent and turn, from this wicked world be
Freed
The flesh it profits nothing, nor friends
Nor family. If you deny to come and be converted, and hang
On your own tree.
Then count your loss as gain, be crucified with Him
Conformed to Christ in suffering, and resurrection in
The end.
What is the point to this dirge, what would I try to say?
The Spirit is life the flesh profits Nothing!
You must be born again . . .
The Spirit 'searches' all things, yes, the deep things of God.
If any man has not the Spirit of Christ,
He belongeth not to God.

You don't have to be;
You don't have to be so Holy you know!
O Yes I Do!
You are just a Holy Joe I don't want to be near you.
That breaks my heart my friend. Would you say that if Jesus just
Happened to walk in?
Well there's more to life than God you know!
No! not that I'm aware of!
Well what about your family?
Well what about my Father's love?
Well your just a radical, that's what I can see!
Well who could be more radical, than someone who would
Choose to die for the likes of you and me?
Well I don't like all this Jesus stuff, and you Pray way to much!
Well I have been with Jesus Christ, and I have felt His Holy touch.
Well that's fine if you think so, but it's not for me.
Well I'm sad to hear that friend. I know from where I've come and been,
And nothing I have ever seen could ever please me but my King.

YOU HAVE THE RIGHT TO REMAIN QUIET!

You have the right to remain quiet!
You have the right to lay down your life, to be crucified with Christ, yet live!
You have the right to view "all" things you thought
gain as loss for the sake of knowing Him!
You have the right to His righteousness,
through the Cross! Not to come to Him in your own ways.
You have the right to die to self, that salvation you might gain.
You have the right to be buried with Him in baptism,
and be raised again in newness of life!
You have the right to eternal life, if you truthfully choose Christ!
You have the right to humble everything of you!
You have the right to turn away from the world that owns you!
You have the right to repent deep down, even to the dirt!
You have the right to cry to God even screaming, that you hurt so deep inside,
where you try to hide, so that no one will ever know
your pride and unbelief. 'He is God not you.'
You have the right to come and cry, cry to understand.
You have the right to seek and pray
that He will make you stand before His throne,
when you're alone and need someone to lean on!
Oh, you have the right!
But if you choose this choice instead,
you'll have the right to sin and self till dead.
And then you'll see so differently, the rights you had you threw away!
Now here's the state that you will find, you will guide your ways
by your own mind, and every day will pass away,
and you will have nothing of heaven's stake.
You'll be left alone to wonder on,
self-deceived, self on your throne,
and you'll soon find, 'reprobate mind,'
there's nothing of God, that you can find
in the landscape of your heart!
The day will come - it does to all,
when down at death's door you shall fall,
and when you arise on judgment day,
then you'll face the one You turned away -
for your own will, friend, or family, whatever it was

No longer will be between you and Him,
when you alone there stripped and bare
will stand before His glorious throne,
He'll say to you, "Now testify!"
You'll tell the truth, and not one lie!
"I had the right to live for Me!
I had the right to be Free!
I had My own philosophies!
I had the right to all of these!
I had the right to my own will!
I had the right to turn from You!
I had the right! to My friends you know!
I had the right! God! To family!
You never heard one of my prayers!
When I was hurt no one was there.
You never told Me that it would be hard!
I didn't believe enough to change My heart,
and mind. And I didn't come to be baptized.
I know I was told without one lie!
I didn't seek your Holiness,
I didn't truly cry out to you - like this!
Now is see what You spoke of, and I truly see
That You are love. I wish I would have listened twice,
instead of following my own lies and alibis!"
Your testimony is now through. Here is the sentence over you.
"Take this one in front of Me, cut her in two, here before Me,
then cast Him away into the pit,
Better they learn the fear of the Lord while they may yet repent!

—I offer No apologies / If Jesus is offended, I repent to Him. If flesh is
offended
Look at your life in respect to the truth of Christ, You, must be born again.
It is with fear and trembling that I have written this, are you bold enough to
really
consider it?

Jeremiah says: We don't know love or hate by what's before us, and that the heart is desperately wicked and evil altogether! All scripture is designed to bring us to the understanding that without the 'REAL being born again of the Spirit' we are dead. And being dead there is No love in us; the love of the flesh, even for kin is the love of lust. Part of the fruit of the tree of the knowledge of good and evil. 'knowledge' Philosophy = the love of knowledge. Pseudo Christian knowledge is as philosophy. It's useless Paul says. The kingdom of God comes with power. So where are we when we know? - Love is Galatians 2:20 crucified with Christ, then to live His life in the power of His Spirit. Jesus said, 'the Spirit is life, the flesh profits nothing,' so too with flesh-that is Human love. If a man of God were to rebuke someone, would that not be love, and if He didn't rebuke because he was desiring no conflict, would that not be hate?

Jesus said: Unless a grain of wheat fall to the ground and dies it remains by itself.

Paul said: Did you receive the Holy Ghost when you believed?

Hubert asks you, Reader: Did yourself die? Did you receive the Holy Ghost when you believed?

Or, Did you come to a false Jesus, a false gospel A Bar- Jesus? Bar-Jesus was Elymas in Scripture, a witch of sorts who always lead people away from the truth. Christ in you is still 'the only' hope of Glory. If your 'faith' does not include dying to self, being crucified with Christ as a seed falling to the ground and die-ing, it is a false faith! If it does not indwell you with the Holy Ghost, convict you of sin, righteousness, and judgment, it is useless, except to condemn you at the last day. If you are Christ's you must know His Spirit and be indwelt with the Spirit of God.

Jesus said: If you do not hate father, mother, husband, wife, brother, sister etc., even your own life, you cannot 'be' My Disciple.

Tell me where your favorite beliefs fit? How do your sentimental feelings, or philosophies, or family, or anything, or anybody fit in this?

If either an Angel, or any man or even we ourselves preach to you any other gospel Paul said: 'Let him be accursed!' Can we catch a glimpse here that the kingdom of God is pretty straight and sure? I guarantee that there will be no doctrine, or Philosophy, or traditions in Glory! It will be Glory because the 'living truth' is there!

Man look out! I want to tell you to throw yourself down at the feet of the Real Jesus, and cast far from you 'yourself' and all your hopes, dreams, desires, fantasies, family-everything. Everything. And God will come as you call on Him in truth and make a new creature of you, a creature made in his image, not yours, or your favorite teacher, or philosopher or whatever…

Seek Him with all your Heart, and Know that He is real.

Entering into the vision I see a silhouette in the darkness. I see the Cross; it is very tall, maybe 20 feet or so. As I am circling the cross, the darkness is turning to a regal, royal blue. I see Jesus on the cross high above the ground. Out of the corner of my eye, still moving to my right, as though the scene before me were on a huge turntable, I see two arms extended forward, covered in a blue robe with deep cuffs. Then I see the Lord's hands, much larger than life now, holding forth His cup. The cup of the covenant of His blood, in His right hand, and in His other hand the bread of life, His broken body.

The earnest of the vision is: This is the bread of life. This is the cup of the covenant of My blood. Will you come? – Will you come?

The covenant of the Lord is the will of the Father. 'I have come to do your will o God,' a body you have prepared for Me. Will you come?- Will you come?

Jesus said If I be lifted up I will draw all men unto Me. Will you come? In John 6:53 He said, "unless you eat of My flesh and drink of My blood you have 'no' life in you." At which point many of His disciples turned away, and walked with Him no more. Will you come? 'Will you?' The kingdom of God does not come by word only, but in power. Will you come? We do not talk our way into the kingdom of God. We must walk the walk of brokenness. Partaking of the true bread of life, and the blood of His covenant, picking up our own cross, and getting on it.

There are no two roads, there are no two paths, there are no cross walks, no two right of ways. The Cross walk of Jesus Christ is the straight, and narrow. It is the Highway of Holiness, Isaiah 35:8-A Highway shall be there, and a road and it shall be called the Highway of Holiness. The unclean shall not pass over it, but it shall be for others. Whoever walks on the road, although a fool, will not go astray.

I awoke from a dream, where I was crucified. I was in the middle of a bunch of people, most of who were watching, while one who hated me nailed me to the cross. The nails were like steel rods and they were big, about an inch in diameter. They hurt bad as he drove them in. The guy who was nailing me to the cross was a big man, and bald headed. He used the hammer which he had driven the rods with to pound on my body while everyone watched, and stood by. He truly loved what he was doing to me 'beating me with that hammer'. And as I was nailed to that cross I could do nothing about it. I could not defend myself. I flew this way, and that way as the blows hit me. After a while, his joy turned to tears, as he began to cry out, "Just deny Him and I'll stop!" But still he continued. I thought I'd die with every blow. There was a sense of death every time he hit or kicked me. He hit me in the head then and everything turned black and peaceful, and I started to feel love for him and to feel sorry for him that I couldn't really help him at all. Still he cried out for me to "just deny Christ" and he was then crying, even hating what he was doing to me. Then everything changed, and there were children around me, taunting me and dancing around me in circles. Some were girls and some were boys. One child seemed to be the worst and I tried to reach out to him, but he would come and taunt me, and touch me. I could feel the Holy Spirit leave me and come right back, and I could feel the boy's curses and evil. Yet the more he did this the more I loved him. Also I felt the more they all hated me and cursed me, that much more God loved me.

Bring me to your cross Lord Jesus! Nail me to it! Nail me to it hard! If someone has to die for this evil generation, let it be me. Let thy will be done Lord, I don't want anything of this world. Come and crucify me with you. There is no greater gain than to suffer for Christ's sake in this world. Everything we lose for His sake is gain to us in glory.
Lord I see this as a call to martyrdom, to self mortification as in Colossians chapter three. So when I am finally done flailing around and trying to run, please wake me up to it and let's get it done.

Is this true? Yes it's true. There is a fire to be kindled. Oh how I wish it were already lit! All self-will and desire is rebellion and the only cure for rebellion is repentance, and our own cross. When a person is crucified with Christ they don't get to choose what happens to them anymore. The cross deals completely with self-will and selfishness, which is Idolatry [witchcraft]

Where does the anointing come from? Being here with you. I will walk the straight and narrow. I will run the rough and rocky road. I will walk the lonely paths to be with you my Lord. When troubles fall upon me, and shadows fall around, when darts and arrows come at me, in your hand Lord 'I'll' be found. Just to be with you I'll give anything, I'll do what it takes, because just to be with you is all that matters. This life is not my own.

I'll go where you send me, just lift my head above my enemy, that wherever I may go or be I will be with you. To be with you is everything.

I know that I'm a soldier, though this is not my war. I know that I've been drafted, but the battle is the Lord's.

The affairs of this wicked world don't matter anymore. I'll sleep just outside my Master's gate waiting for my Lord,

How can I do any other, even finding my own pleasure while my Master wages battles for my eternal soul?

As He says to me watch and pray lest you fall into temptation. And fall away from the Lord.

When the Angel of His presence touches your Heart, it is not as though it were a naked little baby with a bow shooting eye fluttering little love darts into men's hearts. No it's like you've been shot through with an arrow, impaled with a spear, or skewered with a sharp two edged sword! And you cry out

OH GOD YOU ARE REAL!

"You Said"

You said you want to be real with God! To know His will and ways.
To come into His Kingdom in reality and truth. God says Okay! Ok,
But it's gonna hurt! Because if you've spent your time entertaining
Your mind, your mind will become a toy rather than a tool.

—Lord come, as I sit and wait for you, my heart waits for your Holy touch,
the breath of life is yours to give, and by your Spirit Lord I live.
My mind is reeling from all this pain, my heart burning from all this shame,
my hands defiled with blood and mire, yet my soul is set on you,
you are my one desire! How can I truly come to you?
How can I come and be renewed?
All manner of snare I've been caught in, and every one of them from sin.
Lord Jesus come and deliver me, cleanse my heart and set my soul and spirit free.
Take my life and draw me near, take my soul and wash it clean.
Come and free me from every snare, The fear of man and this worlds care,
The shame of all of my own sin. Lord I confess, please wash me deep within.
Turn my sickness into health, turn my poverty to wealth, my lack
Father turn to gain, my sin and shame please wash away again.
I pray Jesus in your Holy name. Amen.

What in the world is there to gain if I don't have your Spirit?
If I don't have your Spirit I have nothing. Jesus you said "the Spirit is life,
The flesh profits nothing" Lord fill me with
your Spirit again and overflow me
With your holy flame I pray in Jesus name.

The Spirit of God is the beauty of Holiness,
the peace of love, and the received grace
For eternal life in Jesus Christ.
The presence of the Person, the Holy Spirit giving
Comfort to a wounded soul, for the spirit is life
the flesh profits nothing! Blessed be His Holy name.

When the day of the Lord comes,
where will His Majesty find 'you?'
One thing I ask Lord, that will I seek,
that I may dwell in the house of the Lord,
To behold the beauty of the Lord and to enquire in His temple.

It is a fearful thing to fall into the hands
of the living God. But far better to fall into
The hands of the living God in sheer terror of Him,
than to not fall into His hands
Until the last day. There is no other place for me!
I want with all my heart to fall into His hands today, to face
His judgment today, while I may be able to repent rather than to risk being
Puffed up with myself in pride risking His eternal judgment
on that day when it's to late!

We have no common ground with God until we are crucified with Christ. For flesh cannot enter the kingdom of God. Therefore we must put off the deeds of the flesh, and all of its desires, being dead to the flesh and alive to God Dead to the world and alive to Christ, For the scripture says, For you Have died and your life is hidden with Christ in God. Therefore it is no longer I who live, but Christ who lives within me. Jesus come! Lord Jesus come! Have mercy on your people, who claim you, but don't know you.

Save those who seek your Kingdom with intensity, and purpose, to truly know you God.

Your Glory is in the Heavens O God, your faithfulness reaches unto to the sky, your righteousness is like the Mighty mountains and I put my trust in you. Oh God you are, Yeah, you are wonderful. Great and greatly to be praised. Father Let your light shine in the heart's of all those who call out to you in truth. Bless your holy name. Jesus you are the only way! the only truth, the only life . . . I . . . there is no other. Help your people to draw near to you. amen.

Your Land Is Filled With Blood Guilt

Your land is filled with blood guilt. 'Pursue peace and Holiness' without which no one shall see the Lord. The blood [guilty of blood] flows thickly throughout your land. Men and women defiling one another, and robbing one another. Sexual immorality is over flowing in every street! Holiness is rejected. And my children are rejected, by all the sorcerers of the Land. It is as though Sodom had revived, and Gomorrah had come to your land. "I am the Lord". Your Men take a fancy to Hype, and cheap and shallow talk. No one takes to heart that I am the Lord, I am a Holy God! A God, who requires 'Holiness' of His children.

Without Holiness No one will see the Lord.

Not one whoremonger, adulterer, fornicator, thief, liar, or greedy person, will ever stand before me. I am not mocked! You're Pastors who do not take my word to heart, but rather seek to fill my house with such as these will not stand before me, they will not minister to me. No, they put out the eyes of those who see, and cast them out of my house. Woe to them. Sodom is their reward, lest they quickly turn and repent.

Because of greed, and the greedy among you, they all lie in wait for the blood of the innocent, the weak, and the poor. Woe to them! 'I am the Lord!' Woe to those who add house to house, who build many more, to house the poor, and then to plunder them while they are in your midst!

Without holiness no one will see the lord.

You travel too, and fro, finding new teachings, and new teachers to heap up for yourselves! Even that they might bring you good news of great and swelling glory! [pride] Yet you cannot stay at home, and mourn for the son of my right hand whom you have destroyed, because you have rejected my voice long ago.

The adulterous woman cannot stay at home either! Nor can she pray, or repent of her running too, and fro looking for a new man! Tell me if this is not you? Do you rather to meet with me, than any other? Are you faithful to hear my voice? Is there another whom you desire? {If I am} you're Husband! Where then is my Honor? Where is my devotion, and love? Are you not a prostitute? Without holiness no one shall see the lord!

Pastors take it to Heart! Stop selling yourselves to the innkeepers, and the rich spoilers who slay my children for a piece of bread! You are covered with blood, while you mock at me, making wide the lips, yes, making jeers, and sneers. I see your Heart! Are you not illegitimate sons? Go on take your stand, mock me to my face, lifting up your hands, preaching, and praying with great pretence, while 'you' do not know me, and cast my words behind you. I see your Heart. I see your desires. I know your deepest thoughts, that they are futile, and you do not take my words to heart. Again I would say to you Repent, and again I say, you don't know what that means.

Who are you who speak for me, to the pleasure of the flesh of men, while I command men everywhere to Repent? Jangle, jangle, like the ankle bracelets of the adulterous woman, is the song of your tongue! You sing your own tune while my sons and daughters mourn, and weep for you. Yes and still the blind lead the blind and many are fallen into the ditch!

Who will harm you if you speak what is true from a heart that is broken, yet steadfast, and sure?
How great is the Lord, How great is the mercy of the Lord? Who relents from doing harm?
Many deceivers have gone out into the world. Many illegitimate sons. Without Holiness no one shall see the Lord.
Yeshua [Jesus] let my bonds be in you. Amen.

Your Light

Your light is life your light is truth
Holiness is the light in you
Grace and purity shining glory, your light
is life

My heart cries out to you so hungry for the true
light of life my Spirit waits each day for
a single breath to breathe of life as you
give me breath

You are the life my saviour and friend there is no
other way my dear no other truth at all there is no
other way brother to lift me up after I fall

I've fallen down into so many snares
You are the life the only one who really cares
please Help me Oh Jesus you are the light of life

Please Help Me

Your Love Is Loss

Your love is loss, without
My cross The love of the flesh
Is the love of lust Selfish and greedy are your desires you lust and do not
have—You require
True love as I love friends
Greater love hath no man than that he lay down his life for his—friends

—*Pioneer: Those who go before, who go aside of the familiar,*
And venture into the unknown—[Hubert's definition]
Those of God's children who are breaking the hard ground
Of dead clods, of entangled, twisted, dogmatic death, of traditionalism,
And formalism - to pursue the truth. And the life of God , 'in the Spirit.'
In the Holy Spirit! Jesus said the Spirit is life the flesh profits nothing!
When Jesus says something is nothing, it's nothing! The Lord is waking those
Who desire Him above all to arise, and follow the lamb wherever He goes.

I desire to be all that He wants me to be, yes a pioneer in a foreign land.
A land of rebels, reprobates. And people of every form of ungodliness.
Jesus use me as a pioneer, for the purpose of establishing your kingdom in
This land, and to set up a Holy banner to your name. Amen.

—Early pioneers—

They were stoned, they were sawn in two, were tempted, were slain with the
Sword. They wondered about in sheepskins, and goat skins, being destitute,
afflicted, tormented, of whom the world was not worthy: -For consider Him
[Jesus]
Who endured such hostility from sinners against Himself, lest you become
discouraged in your souls. You have not resisted to bloodshed striving against
sin.; Jesus who in the days of His flesh , when He had offered up prayers and
supplications, With vehement cries and tears to Him who was able to save
Him from death, and was heard because Of His Godly fear, though He was a
son, yet He learned obedience through the things Which He suffered. — It is a
fearful thing to fall into the hands of the Living God. But far better to fall into
the hands of God in sheer terror of Him now, than to not fall into His hands
until your last day! There is no other place for me. I want to fall into His hands
Today! To face Him today! While I may be able to repent! Better this than to
risk being Puffed up with self, and pride risking His eternal judgment on that
day; When it's to late!

Cornerstone to life is death, even the death of the cross! Which Jesus paid for us.
So it doesn't matter if a person is seven, or seventy. Life begins at the cross! For
I am crucified with Christ and yet I live, and the life that I now live, I live by
the Faith of the son of God! So to live is Christ, and to die is gain. We therefore
have no common ground with God, until we are crucified with Christ, Buried
with Him in baptism, and raised into the newness of life, the life of the Spirit.

For flesh and blood cannot enter the kingdom of God. Therefore we must put off the deeds of the flesh, and all of its desires, being dead to the flesh and alive to God. Dead to the world and alive to Christ, scripture says, we have died. And our life is hidden with Christ in God. Therefore it is no longer I who live but Christ who lives within me! Jesus, Come, Have mercy on your people, who claim you, but don't know you Save those who seek your kingdom with Intensity, and purpose to truly know their GOD! Amen.

Get Published, Inc!
Thorofare, NJ 08086
29 January, 2010
BA2010029